Vanished Landmarks

of

North Devon

Typeset by Lens Typesetting, Bideford
Printed by Maslands, Tiverton
Published by North Devon Books

ISBN 0946 290 237

Contents

Old Northam Burrows Lifeboat House, alongside Royal North Devon Golf Club greens.

Vanished Landmarks of North Devon

What inspires an author to suddenly decide upon a title, and a new project? How does it come to fruition – from a germ of an idea to a published volume? A book such as this involves endless research – literally – endless pursuing of individuals who may or may not be able to help and many hours ruining one's eyesight pouring over the small print of the yellowing pages of the Bideford Gazettes and the Journal Heralds of yesteryear.

Many of you will have read 'Vanished Houses of North Devon', published many years ago now, but still in print, and still popular. Those houses disappeared for largely economic and social reasons. Since writing it, I have become increasingly aware that many other familiar sights have gone, or are in danger of going. Many of the landmarks of the older generation have gone irrevocably, and it is amazing how quickly they are forgotten. It may be that the youngsters don't care about their surroundings in the same way, aren't bothered about what has come down, been sacrificed to make way for new roads, new development, or simply succumbed to old age.

'It's had its day – so what?' could be the general attitude. I hope this book may seek to alter that and to gently point out that in many instances the loss has been tragic and even unnecessary, and the replacement by no means always an improvement.

Many of the landmarks have been lost through natural forces, fire in many instances, the tragic Lynmouth floods, but the majority have been removed by man's overzealous hand. It is only in recent years that those in power have come to appreciate what is now loosely dubbed "our heritage" and legislation has required that some semblance of consideration is paid to preservation. In fairness, what one generation happily consigns to the scrapheap, another fights tooth and nail to preserve. The cannons of good taste are as elusive as ever and striking a happy balance seems an impossibility.

Whilst acknowledging the impracticability of preserving everything, this book does, at least, hope to preserve a record of what has been lost. And the list is long and sad, with the desecration of our towns a particularly sad story. Here it was difficult to know what to incude and what to leave out. Many small buildings, shops, alleys etc. have been flattened in the path of progress – all too often for car parks or multi-store schemes, and everyone has their pet passion. But these are not really landmarks, in the true sense of the word. They were the bread and butter of our surroundings; the landmarks were the jam and cream. And far too many have gone. I could have gone on forever, or so it seemed at one stage, and even as I was writing, the large house at the entrance to the Northam Burrows – Sandymere or Pimpley Gate — it used to be called, disappeared in two short days, the victim of a bulldozer and a redevelopment plan. The limekilns at Buck's Mills are threatened, which is a disgraceful state of affairs, and it is difficult to say what well known and loved feature may be the next to come under some unlooked for threat.

It is largely the losses of this century that are included – those that many can still remember, or at least recall their passing. Railway nostalgia is catered for elsewhere, and could have filled a whole book on its own, so the railways themselves have been left alone – and fortunately many of their more spectacular landmarks, such as the Chelfham Viaduct, are still with us.

Is it the passing of time that gives that which we have lost an aura of attractiveness? And is it the old adage that comparisons are odious that makes the modern replacements seem so brash, so mundane – often so tawdry? Will a future generation mourn the passing of, say, the Civic Centre in Barnstaple? Is there the same affectionate feeling for the new North Devon District Hospital that enabled the NDI to be supported entirely by public subscription? Will people keep up a 24-hour vigil to preserve some well-loved feature in the same way that one man protected the last of the trees on Bideford Quay from the developers?

Before all is lost – including the contemporary records – this book sets out to provide some kind of record. At times it is incomplete – memories have already proved unreliable, or records have been lost – and hopefully many people will contact me with the missing clues so that a further edition may be remedied. But at least it is something – and no doubt it will stir memories for some of you.

A remarkable photograph of Northam windmill

Researching into past history is always fascinating — and the golden rule of never allowing oneself to be sidetracked is almost always ignored. Half-forgotten oddments, unknown and obscure, claim attention and distract, however strong-minded the original intention. Time ceases to have any meaning and one item leads to another, like a detective unravelling a chain of clues. In fact there is great similarity, and the question "What do you want to know?" is the hardest of all to answer.

Browsing through old newspapers can be most rewarding — and most frustrating. The oldest editions are full of national, and even international, news and local news has to vie with sovereign remedies for strange ailments, and items such as a Glasgow murder case, a foreign skirmish, and Parliamentary reports. More recent editors, having been relieved of the duty of covering such a wide stage, turned to interminable wedding reports, council and court almost verbatim, and long columns dealing with the local markets. But they are the most valuable record we have — and without them books such as this would be virtually impossible. Today's editors have a heavy responsibility to continue the tradition.

The yellowing, fragile pages hold a wealth of local history; dates, facts, pictures — all so easily lost when relying on private individuals, and even museums, where what one person holds dear represents so much old clutter to someone else. Even local authorities, since reorganisation in 1974 seem to have lost all knowledge of their files and records. Endless 'phone calls and "passing the buck" technique leads nowhere.

Thank goodness for the local record office in Barnstaple, and the Athenaeum, the Ilfracombe Museum and Library, and the Bideford archive, where much valuable material is not only stored, but readily available to all. For the sake of future researchers, and future generations, might I put in a personal plea to all of you who have old documents and photographs, to lodge them with one of these estimable keepers before they are lost for all time?

The year 1952 proves a good example of how items come to light, unexpectedly and unsought. This was the year that Yelland Power Station was completed and it was for accounts of this that I was turning the pages of the Bideford Gazette. It was a momentous year – King George VI died and his daughter began her long reign. Then the wet summer culminated in the disastrous Lynmouth floods. There were several progress reports on Yelland – and two other items not to the forefront of my mind well rewarded my patient search. The first was the account of the final days of Chanter's Folly. But following on the next week, a reader sent in an account, plus picture, of the old windmill between Northam and Appledore. This is the only account I have come across, and that afternoon off I went with dog and son to see what there was to be discovered.

Most people assume that Windmill Lane in Northam, at the bottom of which are the old Northam UDC offices in which the Bideford archive is now housed, leads to the site of the windmill. And it is surprising how few local people remember it. Yet it must have been a very prominent landmark. And large chunks of it still exist. From the far end of Windmill Lane looking across the top of Knapp House, what looks like a ruined farmbuilding can be seen on the highest point of the field opposite. A footpath leads from Bidna Lane over the top of this field, past the ruins, and down to the next lane, leading to Appledore.

The ruins are the base of the old windmill, and presumably the footpath existed to serve the mill. Certainly it is little used today. Stone-built, it appears to have been rectangular, with a sturdy opening in the north-west wall. A few remnants of brick lie around. It is a marvellous airy spot with views all round – over Westward Ho! to Clovelly and Hartland Point, across the estuary to Saunton Sands, and out over Appledore and the Burrows.

The report in the 1952 Gazette states that in 1922 Mr Cork of Watertown Farm, Appledore, on whose land the derelict windmill stood, contracted for the tower to be taken down. It was by then a dangerous ruin and he was concerned for his cattle. He stipulated that no gunpowder was to be used as a previous attempt in 1908 has resulted in damage to Knapp House. Digging operations commenced and the sides collapsed. The contractor then laid a single charge that night and by the next morning only a heap of rubble remained.

The tower was a substantial brick-built structure, and it was reported that the mortar used was of such strength that it was impossible to separate the bricks. The tower collapsed in sections. Mr Cork had these removed — and to those who walk along the coastal footpath between the Appledore Gate to the Burrows and Hinks' yard, they form a prominent protective wall to the field that fronts Watertown farm. The red brick stands out from the surrounding pebbles, and the sections have been cemented together to form a sturdy wall — so that the Northam windmill survives to this day!

Cr-r-u-m-p-h !

LAST PICTURES OF CHANTER'S FOLLY

Regretted . . . but old father Torridge rolls on

The pictures above and alongside show the demolition of Chanter's Folly on Thursday of last week. Alongside is seen the partly-dismantled tower with workmen passing around the stump the cable which was pulled by a bull-dozer to effect the demolition. The "battle scene" above shows the bull-dozer battering the remainder of the tower level and clearing the site.

Below, sunshine and shadow . . . the old tower has gone, its sentinel-like duty finished, but the Torridge, which it overlooked for so many years, reflect

9

An oil painting of the Shebberton race course by Major Moore

Few of those who walk across the short turf of the cliffs at *Abbotsham* have any idea that it ever had any past other than as a sheep run. Yet the valley that runs inland from the cliffs, and the cliffs themselves, have a few secrets, now almost entirely forgotten and almost entirely vanished without trace.

"The most beautifully situated race course in England" was how the Tatler magazine described the small course at Shebberton. And if one man's schemes had reached maturity, then the headland and the village might have had a very different story to tell, and could well have changed irrevocably from quiet unspoilt fields and cliffs to all the bustle and development that accompany horse meetings and racing events.

Mr Skidmore Ashby of Rixlade was the *"moving star in the excellent organisation which created the first properly laid out race course in North Devon."*

The course was laid out in the valley below the footpath that crosses the fields from Abbotsham Court, and extended almost to the cliff edge. It was properly and professionally constructed using white painted rails to Tattersalls standards, with a judge's box and a clubhouse and changing rooms.

An account comes from the Bideford Gazette of the first race meeting on 27th September, 1922:

"It is admirably situated, giving a magnificent view of the Bay from Croyde to Hartland Point with Lundy in the distance and with a vantage position for spectators to obtain uninterrupted views of the racing from start to finish. The actual course runs along the valley of Abbotsham Court and Cornborough and is practically level except for a gentle slope rising to the straight run home."

The one-and-a-quarter-mile course was scheduled for pony and Galloway races and as the Pony and Galloway Racing Association had come to an end in 1918, rules were specially drawn up. It was hoped the races would give a fillip to the breeding of ponies and Galloways in the district.

The first race meeting, it was reported, was a brilliant success that augured well for the future. The day was fine apart from "an ungallant shower of rain during the ladies' race" and "dozens of motor chars-a-bancs, motor cars and vehicles of all descriptions", crowded the site.

There was music from the members' enclosures and "a large number of bookmakers." Stakes amounted to £150 and the races had names with a local flavour – the Westward Ho! Stakes, the Abbotsham Plate, the Bideford Plate, the Shebbertown Club Cup, the Ladies' Hunt Cup and the Farmers' Plate.

The setting was beautiful and the siting ideal. "There is no other race course in England where spectators can enjoy a start to finish view without the aid of stands".

The situation was undoubtedly admirable — but it led to the failure of the course as a financial project. A public right of way has always existed from the entrance to Abbotsham Court to the cliffs, and it was impossible to prevent the locals from making use of free vantage points. From the cliffs at Cornborough, reached from Westward Ho! there was also an uninterrupted view of the race course. After only two seasons, and with failing health, Mr Ashby decided not to continue. The course was dismantled and apart from a few greyhound races, the turf reverted to purely agricultural use.

Mr Ashby had been the moving force in the formation of the National Pony Turf Club. Together with a retired Brigadier General formerly with the Indian cavalry and with racing experience at the Calcutta Turf Club, and a Major with similar experience in Australia and New Zealand, strict rules were drawn up for pony racing, and it was hoped to gain the recognition of the Jockey Club, or the National Hunt Committee. The club also held meetings at Exeter, Bude, Wadebridge, Crediton, Weymouth, Gunnislake and Ottery St Mary — and at Greenford Park in Middlesex. (Mr Ashby came from Staines in Middlesex.) Failure to gain recognition of either body was another contributary reason for the closure of the course, and the end of the National Pony Turf Club. Had it succeeded and continued to gain in popularity, pony racing might by now have formed a major popular sport.

The demise of the race course was a particular disappointment to the owners of arab horses in the area, as this breed had been prominent in the racing programme and it had been hoped to attract more arabs as the course became better known, and arabs and Abbotsham become synonymous.

The only tangible remains are the tall double gates where the footpath to the cliffs leaves the lane and the footpath itself, raised on to a causeway across the marshy field. These were the principal entrances for horses and spectators, and the concrete base of the turnstile, evaded by so many, remains inside the grounds of the Old Race Course Bungalow. This was the former clubhouse and refreshment rooms, with a verandah overlooking the course.

Mr Skidmore Ashby

A little higher up the cliffs were another group of buildings — it must have been quite crowded down on the beach earlier this century! Very few traces remain of what were quite substantial buildings. Continual rock slips, rough winters and probable plundering of the stonework have led to their almost total disappearance with only a level platform and a few steps giving a clue. Considering how prominent they were and how familiar a site they must have been to the many locals who visited the beach, surprisingly few records exist.

Mr George Taylor moved to Abbotsham Court in 1871. He was a railway engineer involved in the construction of the Bideford to Westward Ho! railway. He built two summerhouses for the use of his family when bathing, and Mr Taylor was also responsible for the odd rectangular rock pool below — his attempt at a pool for use when the tide was out. A circular cabin made from a ship's funnel was equipped with a stove for cooking and its rusting shape could be seen until fairly recently. The pool remains, but the huts and the wooden steps that led down to the beach disappeared some time

A postcard view of Abbotsham cliffs

The same view taken in the late 1960's

early this century.

Below the site of these huts are the fast vanishing remnants of some much earlier buildings. A fireplace and substantial chimney built into the cliff occasioned much comment from visitors. After all, fireplaces half way up cliffs are not exactly commonplace!

A newspaper article written in 1968 describes them.

"Still to be seen, however, in the side of the cliffs immediately below the site of Taylor's house are curious remains of buildings of a much earlier date. These are of stone and mortar, set right into the cliff face. On the one hand there is a large open-hearthed fireplace, with a chimney flue leading upwards from it. Facing it, across the recess in the cliffs, are thick walls, obviously the remains of some other building. To the seaward side of the fireplace further walling can be seen, partly faced with pebbles.

An old photograph, taken somewhere around the year 1900, which shows the cliff-top structures, also shows these remains in some detail, although by then they were obviously in disuse. The chimney can be seen as part of an open-ended building, probably a boathouse. Why, one wonders, should a boathouse have had such a massive fireplace and chimney?"

The writer, Mrs Helen Harris, suggests that these may have been built by local fishermen who used them for smoking or cooking the quantities of shellfish to be caught on the beach.

The origins of the pebble-faced seawall at the base of the cliffs is harder to unravel, unless it was simply built to protect the fishermen's equipment. The suggestion that it formed part of a quay seems unlikely, even taking into account the possibility that the beach a hundred years ago could have been some fifteen feet higher than it is today.

Within a few more years all will be gone and the scores of walkers who now tramp the coastal footpath will have no idea of the activity that once existed on this now deserted clifftop turf.

During the last war the fields that made up the race course were trenched to prevent possible enemy aircraft landing there. Evidence of this has now mostly disappeared, as have the corrugated iron huts that once existed on the cliff edge.

These were ex-army huts and were erected by Mr Ashby in 1922, and were used by holiday makers, and by the occasional tramp, one of whom used to capitalize on his situation by picking the mushrooms from the fields, and then knocking at the back door to sell them back to their rightful owners!

Close-by, and more in evidence than the other by-gones was a rifle range, much used for war-time practice, but discontinued following complaints from locals.

On the far side of the valley is the scar of another vanished landmark — the old Bideford to Westward Ho! railway. It was already gone by the time the racecourse came into being, or the two might have helped each other survive, with racing specials run from Bideford on race days. The railway closed during the 1914-18 War, never to reopen. Traces of it can be found in several places around the district but nowhere is such a length of line so plainly evident as here running out to Cornborough. Passengers really would have had a grand stand view!

Lifeboat Houses

This interesting photograph appeared in the pages of Country Life Magazine in March, 1977. The accompanying letter stated that the

"gaunt ruin was a considerable landmark midway along the Pebble Ridge when the snapshot was taken in April, 1913. One half was sufficiently high to house a lifeboat with mast, and the upper storey of the other half, with chimney stacks, probably provided quarters for the crew".

The writer continued that there was no trace of a slipway and he doubted, correctly, if there ever had been one. Interestingly he continues:

"When lifeboat stations of this type were built I do not know. This one had, clearly, been long abandoned. Probably it had been supplanted in Victorian days, as the Ordnance Survey of 1900 marks a lifeboat station in a more suitable site at the extreme northern end of the Pebble Ridge."

17

In a letter of reply to Country Life, Graham Farr of the Lifeboat Enthusiasts' Society stated that the first house was replaced in 1856, and this was altered several times to accommodate larger lifeboats. There were doors at both ends so that the boats could be pushed out bow first at high water or taken by horses at low water, travelling across the sand to the closest point to the ship in distress.

The horses used for launching were kept at the farm opposite Hinks' boatyard, and it is said they would jump the hedge and gallop to the Boathouse when they heard the maroon.

In 1889, the lifeboat moved back to Appledore, to the same site occupied by the RNLI boathouse today. The old boathouse remained, deteriorating fast in the exposed conditions of the Atlantic coast, and was finally demolished in 1913. All that remains, close to the seventh green, are a concrete platform and a few grassy mounds. The golf club have named the eighth green after the lifeboat, or perhaps the first writer was right, and there were two sites?

In the days when the old lifeboat house was built, oars and muscle were the only form of power available. Prior to 1852 the early lifeboats had been housed close to Appledore, but on several occasions the strength of the tide combined with rough seas and gale force winds made it impossible for the lifeboat to force its way down the estuary and across the notoriously dangerous Bar. It is amazing that the six-man crew performed this feat at all, and then continued to battle with mountainous seas to carry out a rescue.

It was decided in 1851 that a new site was needed for the lifeboat house and it was reported in July of that year that the Royal National Institution for the Preservation of Life from Shipwreck had granted the sum of £30 towards the erection of a new house "at the back of North Burrows as a more convenient and desirable spot for keeping the lifeboats in."

Early in August The Rev J H Grossett, Mr T B Chanter, the Lloyds agent, and Mr E M White, the architect, visited the Burrows to decide upon the exact spot

"on which to erect a building for the custody of the Bideford lifeboats, that in cases where they may be called for they shall be launched

and sent to the rescue of the unfortunate in much less time than heretofore. In the building every convenience will be at hand for those who may require restoratives ..."

And on 6th November the same year it was recorded that the North Devon Humane Society for the Preservation of Life from Shipwreck laid the foundation stone of their third repository for their boats. Bad weather prevented Lord Fortescue from attending, but Lord Ebrington (his son) and the Hon Dudley Fortescue "buffeted the prevailing storm together with the committee and a sprinkling of ladies" to lay the first stone.

It is perhaps worth recording that the chairman of the Appledore Lifeboat branch was the Reverend Gosset, vicar of Northam, who twelve years later founded the North Devon Golf Club with a committee almost entirely consisting of lifeboat committee members. Perhaps they were already playing there, and no doubt the lifeboat house made a useful shelter when bad weather caught the players at the furthest extremity on the golf course,

In 1846 it was decided to station a lifeboat at Airy Point on the Braunton side of the estuary and for over 70 years a lifeboat house existed across the estuary on Braunton Burrows. This was considered the solution to the problem of crossing the Bar before the Northam Burrows boathouse was built. That at Braunton was operational from 1848. But there were difficulties. It was a long way from Braunton and the men and horses had to travel several miles to the boathouse before they could begin to launch. The boat was manned by an Appledore crew who rowed across.

The maintenance of the three lifeboat stations seems to have been a costly item, and in May, 1860, it was reported that over £1,000 had been spent.

This did not prevent the building of a further lifeboat house at Braunton, which was opened in November, 1862. Apparently it

"replaced a most confined and ill-suited house having no room to turn when the lifeboat was inside. Probably there is not a more deserted spot on the whole coast than that on which the new house has been erected."

The cost was £232, £120 of which was raised locally.

In all, there were six lifeboats supported by the Barnstaple and Braunton RNLI branch, formed in 1862, including three 'Robert & Catherine's. The Braunton boat was launched when it was too rough for the Appledore boat. Three guns were fired, and the keeper at the White House fired three rockets. Men and horses got together on their way out to the lifeboathouse and prepared to launch the boat whilst the crew rowed across the estuary.

Ten horses were used to tow the carriage on which the lifeboat rested into the water. An interesting account comes from S E Ellacott's book on "Braunton Ships and Seamen" where he describes the method used to launch – with ten horses individually harnessed, five aside. On reaching the water, the tracks were removed, the horses wheeled round so that the lifeboat went in bow first, and the horses fanned out clear of the boat as she floated off.

Closure came in 1919. There was a shortage of horses and men as a result of the War, and the boat at Appledore was considered adequate!

Braunton Lifeboat House

The Braunton lighthouse was erected in 1822 and lasted until 1959 when it was replaced with steel girder tower.

The old hospital ship at Broadsands. It served as an isolation hospital – apparently only used once, and sold for scrap in 1927.

Westward Ho! Pier

No Victorian seaside resort was complete without a pier. The founding fathers of Westward Ho! were determined that their speculative venture should be no exception. Development of Westward Ho! as a premier holiday resort had begun in 1863 and whilst the grand hotels, the villas of the wealthy and the tall blocks of apartments and boarding houses were still being built, plans were made for that crowning glory decreed by fashion, and the Northam Burrows Promenade and Landing Pier Company was floated — if that's the right word — in 1864. Their plans were ambitious. The pier was to be 600 feet in length, with a refreshment house and a bandstand on the pierhead.

It took until 1870 to get the necessary Act of Parliament and to raise sufficient capital. Work was commenced by the firm of Gooch, a name well known in the engineering world, and the builders of Bognor Regis pier in Sussex. Work went ahead with the equivalent of a foundation stone-laying ceremony performed by Mrs Moore Stevens, wife of the High Sheriff. She nailed the first plank in place!

By July, 1871, the pier had advanced sufficiently far out into the water for an organised landing to take place. Several small rowing boats ferried passengers from a Bideford vessel to the pier — amidst cheers and champagne, according to a newspaper report.

The same newspaper fuelled enthusiasm by unleashing all kinds of possibilities. Journeys, or rather voyages, could be contemplated across to Swansea, up the Channel to Bristol, overseas to Ireland, and by landing at Ilfracombe could save many road miles. It could also be used as a landing stage when the Bar was too rough, or the tides wrong. There was even talk of the resort having its own steamer to make full use of the pier.

Unfortunately, this optimism was short-lived. A savage gale in October, 1871, snapped the cast iron pillars, leaving only the first 150 feet undamaged.

The contract was redrawn and taken over by the Bideford firm of W & J Abbott, who consolidated what was left and opened the pier to the public in July, 1873.

It looks an attractive structure, with the two little pavilions at the shore end, and a turnround at the far end. A pony pulled a small basket carriage up and down for those without the energy to walk and, for a while, the pier enjoyed a small measure of popularity. But it was never much of a financial success, and ultimately had to be sold to the development company of Westward Ho! to pay off outstanding debts. The pier gradually declined, although it was still popular with swimmers who dived off the end, and with fishermen who found it a great boon. But year by year it became shabbier as the elements took their toll.

During the winter of 1880, another storm snapped some of the pillars, and the owners decided enough was enough. They cut their losses and dismantled the structure the following spring, leaving the two rows of iron stumps marching out into the sea, visible as the tide recedes, and causing much comment among the more observant holidaymakers.

Woody Bay Pier

Some twenty years later another developer had the same idea
— and would have been considerably better off had he learnt the
lessons of Westward Ho! Not only did Benjamin Lake end up
broke, he also landed in jail. His scheme was to develop the
peaceful, wooded retreat of Woody Bay into a small resort, and
since the area was not easy to reach by road, and since he sought to
attract the lucrative trade of the pleasure steamers that in those
days plied the Bristol Channel from the Welsh coast and Bristol
itself, he looked upon a pier as a necessity, rather than a luxury.

Woody Bay is more sheltered than the exposed coastline of
Westward Ho! and the tremendous rise and fall of the tide meant
that the pier needed to be high rather than long. Work commenced in 1896 but was dogged by misfortune from the start.
Neither Lake nor his grandiose ideas were popular with the
handful of cottagers who then lived at Woody Bay, and had no
desire to see their peaceful valley developed into a bustling resort,
and since many of them were fishermen, feared their livelihood was
in jeopardy. Numerous stories surround the building of the pier,
one of which is that the locals managed somehow to sabotage the
structure right from the start — perhaps working between the tides
at night time — and it was the section closest to the pierhead that
suffered most damage from an early storm. The plans were
otherwise well drawn up, and both the road specially constructed
to serve the pier, and the concrete pierhead itself survive, proving
that the special concrete devised did indeed survive the impact of
salt water. It had to be quick-setting between the tides — and
hydraulic lime provided the answer.

Disaster dogged the arrival of the first boat in April 1897.
The temper of the two pressmen who eventually landed was not
improved by the driving rain, and by having to be put ashore by
rowing boat because there was insufficient water alongside the
pier!

The hotel was built, and many of the villas that today are such
attractive properties at Woody Bay, but nothing could save the pier

— or Mr Lake. For it was not his own money that had gone into the development, but that of his clients, and he had managed to lose around £170,000. The courts gave him twelve years in which to reflect upon his misdeeds. In 1902, the year after he began his sentence, the pier was finally demolished and sold for scrap, having been partially destroyed in a gale in 1899.

At one time it was equipped with a crane for lifting passengers baggage from the ships, and for the few short years of its life must have been a pleasant port of call for the steamers. But the undertow of the tides was considerable and it went the way of so many piers. The cost of repair never equalled the returns, and so the owners were faced with ever diminishing returns, or cutting their losses and demolishing the brave efforts of our all-conquering ancestors who saw no reason why the sea should not obey them and be included in their general scheme of improving and developing everything around them.

The storm damaged pier

A passenger steamer at Woody Bay

Few people living remember *Hartland Quay,* for by 1925 it had all but disappeared, leaving behind the cluster of buildings that serve as the hotel and museum, and the slipway down to the beach. It is just possible to follow the line of the protective wall where it snaked out into the sea, and a few years ago this was marked with white paint for the sharpsighted.

No-one knows exactly when it was built, but the earliest references to a quay occur in the 17th century, and the first records in the 1830's. Hartland itself is a large parish, remote from the rest of Devon and poorly served by roads. It was a not unreasonable idea to provide the parish with its own harbour to bring goods in and out by sea, and provide a much needed refuge from the Atlantic gales. It was the only haven between Bude and the Bristol Channel. Perhaps the Stucleys, owners of much of the parish, saw the chance of some additional income as well as the convenience of having their own harbour.

Although it was shortlived, it served the community well, and a wide variety of goods were both imported and exported. The buildings huddled against the cliff were once the homes of the fishermen and labourers, with storerooms, a brewery, and the attendant exciseman's headquarters. At one time there was even a bank, and the Hartland Quay five pound note is a much-prized possession.

In 1887 the harbour wall was breached, and for some reason was not repaired, so that each storm added to the damage, and by 1893 it had become unsafe. A severe gale in 1896 sealed its fate and the greater part went completely, leaving only a short stump, which gradually vanished, until by 1925 it was no more.

Prominent in many of the old prints of the quay is the massive limekiln. This, too, has all but vanished, probably robbed for its building stone, but the base of the kiln is still evident.

HARTLAND QUAY as it appeared after the 1896 gale.

HARTLAND. Ruins of Old Pier.

Only the base remains of what must once have been the most conspicuous landmark of the Torridge, and indeed of the Taw, estuary.

The *Clevland monument* was a stone obelisk some fifty feet tall, built on the highest point in front of Tapeley Park, at Westleigh, from which vantage point there is an uninterrupted view of the two estuaries, and out over the Bar to Bideford Bay.

The obelisk commemorated the sad loss at the age of 21 of the young heir of Tapeley, Archibald Clevland, who died as a result of wounds incurred at Inkerman in 1854.

"This pillar was erected by general subscription as a sincere and lasting tribute of affectionate regret for one who will ever remain endeared to the hearts of all who knew him."

It points to heaven
a better and happier Inheritance
than that left behind him here;
and bids all who read these lines
to revere his memory and emulate
his virtues

Sacred
to the immortal memory of Archibald Clevland esq of Tapeley Park

So reads the inscription on one side of the base — all that now remains of the obelisk.

The inscriptions on the other sides complete the sorry tale of young Archibald's loss:

"I have fought a good fight, I have finished my course, I have kept the faith." 2nd Timothy 4th Chapter 7th verse

At the commencement of the late war with Russia, he accompanied the British army to the Crimea, was engaged at the Battle of the Alma and in the heroic and ever memorable charge of the Light

Cavalry Brigade at Balaclava, which stands unparalleled in the history of the World, when after attacking the Russian army in front, and conquering all before them, they found themselves enclosed by an overwhelming force in the rear; again charging with fearful loss, he with two other officers, of his Regiment alone survived. It was then, his horse being severely wounded that this "young hero" was attacked by three Cossacks (the intended aim of the first he averted, the second drove his lance most providentially against his pouch-box, the third having but a blunted weapon inflicted little injury) and with difficulty reached the camp, but a few days after fell mortally wounded at Inkerman, the 5th November, 1854, and was buried with funeral honours on Cathcarts Hill, near Sebastopol.

He was kind and gentle, generous and brave, possessing a courage beyond his years and during the short period of his military service gained the esteem and commendation of his Commanding and Brother Officers while tears of heartfelt sorrow were shed over his honoured remains by those who had so recently faced with him the cannon's mouth and deplored – Oh! how deeply by his widowed mother and bereathed sisters.

The obelisk was the victim of a freak thunderstorm in the summer of 1932, when a thunderbolt toppled it. Lady Rosamund Christie described the storm to the Bideford Gazette;

"While the storm was at its height", she said, "There was a loud fizz, followed almost simultaneously by the loud crack of the lightening and the tremendous crash of the obelisk falling in pieces. I have only heard the fizz once before and that was during a violent storm in the Bavarian Alps. At first we did not realise it was the obelisk and began inspecting the buildings, until someone came running in to say that the monument had gone and then we saw the extent of the damage. There has been no other damage, except for some trees in the grounds which I understand have been struck by lightening. If the cost is not too high I shall rebuild the obelisk although probably not the iron railings that surround it."

"When the lightning struck the obelisk some of the huge blocks of granite with which it was constructed were hurled at a distance of 100 feet, and in falling became embedded in the ground, whilst the iron railings were burnt and twisted into fantastic shapes. Fragments of railings and masonry were scattered in all directions."

Lady Rosamund mentioned that Archibald was an unlucky name in the Clevland family for a cousin of the same name was drowned at sea, and there was a legend that long before news of his death was received, his mother, who was living at Tapeley, had seen him in a dream standing in the doorway of her bedroom with the water dripping from his clothes.

A memorandum sent to his mother reads:

Archibald Cleveland Esq., joined the 17th Lancers from the 7th Dragoon Guards early in 1854; and accompanied his new corps to Turkey in April of that year, and in September following he went with the expedition (on board the ship London with me) to the Crimea. He was present at the affair of Bangleruck on the 19th and the battle of Alma the following day. On the 25th October he was one of the renowned 500 in the ever memorable Battle of Balaklava where he immortalised himself by his cool and dauntless bravery. "He hewed his way" with sword in hand he slew three of the enemy, cutting his way through a large body of men and miraculously came out of the fight on foot (his horse being killed) amidst withering fire of cannon and musketry. On the 5th November following a day of painful recollection, he was by my side at Inkerman, that terrible fight of eight hours and a half where for 5 hours 8000 brave men headed by our noble Duke of Cambridge repulsed the rolling masses of 40,000 Russians and kept them at bay till aided by the French in the final rout of the enemy. He was silent to my observation on the work of human slaughter before us, evidentally reflecting upon the awful charge at hand for which a presentiment seemed to prepare him. A shell from the Russian Frigate 'Thadina' burst on our left front a portion of which severed his sword belt and entered that part of his body (other portions killed one man and one horse and wounded two other men) and he died at 5 am the following morning regretted, esteemed and beloved by all who knew his amiable disposition, faithful bravery and private virtues, fully testified by the tearful eyes of the poor soldiers and Officers who stood over his grave on the 6th (the same day), from the Paymaster, John Stephenson major.

Inscription on his grave:
In memory of Archibald Clevland Esq
of Tapeley Park
Cornet in the 17th Lancers
The only son of the late Augustus and Margaret Caroline Clevland
Born 10th May 1833
died from wounds caused by the bursting of a shell
November 6th 1854
Aged 21 years

Archibald was the only son of Colonel Augustus Saltren Willett, who had inherited Tapeley from his great uncle John Clevland, who died childless in 1817. Colonel Willett was the grandson of one of John Clevland's sisters, and changed his name to Clevland upon inheriting. His wife, Archibald's sorrowing mother, was Margaret Chichester from Arlington.

The male line being broken again, the Tapeley estates passed to Archibald's sister Agnes who, in 1855, married William Langham Christie, and thus Tapeley became part of the Christie Estates, and linked with the Glyndebourne opera house in Sussex, where the family have preferred to live for at least two generations. The current heir, Hector Christie, has recently taken up residence at Tapeley, and he, too, plans to restore the monument 'if it doesn't prove too costly.'

What a marvellous sight that would be, to once again see a graceful stone obelisk soaring high into the sky above the waters of the estuary.

An early photograph of the monument

After the 1932 storm – canon still place

Across the river, almost exactly opposite Tapeley, there was another landmark, built for more mundane purposes and much less graceful, but nevertheless prominent and eye catching for all that.

Chanter's Folly, as it became known, was a sturdy tower built in 1841 by a local shipping owner. Pictures show a stone-built castellated structure looking very much like a church tower, but without the attendant church.

Thomas Chanter was a prominent Appledore man who had been instrumental in the building of the first quay at Appledore, thus greatly improving the facilities of the fishing village which at that time was an important centre for boat building. The tower was built as a signal tower, so that Chanter's returning ships could be sighted as they crossed the Bar and the workmen on Bideford Quay could be alerted in readiness to discharge the vessel, as harbour dues were based on length of time a vessel was moored alongside. Time was money, even then, and harbour charges costly.

There is no certain reason for its nickname of "folly." One legend states that Thomas Chanter climbed to the top of his newly completed tower to watch the homecoming of one of his merchant-men, commanded by his son. Instead he witnessed its shipwreck on the Bar, with the loss of all hands. Another story claims that it was not possible to see the flags used for signalling from Bideford Quay, and that the structure was therefore a 'piece of folly'. He may, however, have intended to signal to Appledore Quay, once it was completed.

As the photographs show, the tower was built near a quarry, and subsequent quarrying operations over the years approached perilously close to the tower. Neglect and storm damage wreaked their toll, so that by the early 1950's it had become badly cracked and highly dangerous.

In October, 1952 Northam Council decided that the tower had become a public danger and informed the owner, Mr Moore of Wooda Farm, that it must come down. The Moore's had already offered the tower to the Council, together with a small piece of land, an offer the Council had declined. Perhaps the report by a firm of Bristol steeplejacks had some bearing on the matter. They considered that it would be possible to stabliise the structure with internal crossing concrete joists, but at a cost of between £1,500 and £2,000, against the demolition costs of around £500 to £800.

Demolition was not going to be easy either. The quarry was partly leased to the Barnstaple Brick and Tile Company, who had a wharf opposite and who used the site for drying their tiles. There were also some cottages in close proximity.

The owners decided to act before the winter set in; on 13th November Chanter's Folly collapsed in a heap of rubble and one of North Devon's most prominent landmarks was no more.

Mr Moore, who owned a small portion of the quarry, had given this, together with the tower, to the tile company, and presumably part of the deal included its demolition. Woolaways were called in (also directors of the tile company) and in a remarkably short space of time the tower had been pulled over and bulldozed into the quarry.

Astonished locals gathered later to mourn its loss and recall the days when it served a useful purpose, and when fairs and celebrations were held in the quarry.

THE DORMY HOUSE, WESTWARD HO! N. DEVON

Next door to the North Devon Golf Club at Northam was the *Dormy House Hotel.* It was a modern building, well situated and apparently prosperous.

Although originally known as the Dormy House, by the 1950's it had changed its name to the Atlanta Hotel, and was advertising golf and putting, horse riding, sand yachting, surfing and water ski-ing as among the activities available. Standing in ten acres, it had a games room, central heating, radios in each bedroom, ample garaging, dancing and was licensed.

On the night of 8th January, 1970, fire broke out. The hotel was closed for the winter and the manager had just completed a programme of redecoration. He and his wife had gone out for the evening. The fire originated at the rear of the hotel and had a good hold by the time it was noticed. Over 60 firemen tackled the blaze, but the entire first floor was gutted. It was fully booked for Easter, and at the time the manager hoped to reopen. In the event, this proved not to be practicable, and the hotel was levelled. A question mark still hangs over the future of the site.

Marland Viaduct

Clay pipes, bricks and sanitary ware were responsible for one of the area's most attractive vanished landmarks. The narrow gauge railway, built to serve the Petersmarland clayworks, crossed the river Torridge below Torrington on an amazing structure of wooden piers and struts. This cats-cradle of timber could surely be described as unique, for there couldn't be another like it, in this country at least.

The clayworks, situated in a remote area between Torrington and Hatherleigh, have existed since at least the 17th century. The increase in the popularity of smoking and Bideford's importance as a port of import for tobacco, led to the rise in demand for the long white clay pipes, and the white ball clay found at Marland was ideal. It was even exported from both Bideford and Fremington. But by the mid 19th century the clay works were in decline, superseded by the more accessible deposits in South Devon. The Rolle canal from Torrington to Landcross ensured that the clayworks did not cease entirely, and the clay was taken downstream by barge to the potteries at Annery (near Weare Giffard).

The upturn came when the North Devon Railway reached Torrington in July, 1872. The owners of the clayworks decided to make use of this new form of transport. With the building boom and industrial expansion of the 19th century, the clay's imperviousness and strength had attracted the attention of the Stafford potteries, and there was quite a demand.

An initial survey for the railway was carried out in 1879, and its construction was allowed to go ahead speedily because it was to be a 'light railway for private use', i.e. the Board of Trade applied lesser standards of building and maintenance. The other favourable factor was that all the landowners along the route gave their permission for the construction of the line, thus saving the need for a costly and time consuming Act of Parliament. The railway was known as the Marland Railway.

The unusual construction of the viaduct was the direct result of the inspired choice of engineer for the line. 'The Green Odd Railway & General Contracting Company Limited' is a somewhat extraordinary name, but it was the company of a highly respected and experienced railway engineer. J B Fell, whose home was at Greenodd in Cumbria, had spent his working life constructing railways across high mountains, in particular Switzerland, and also pioneered a centre-rail system used by the mountain railway on the Isle of Man.

The first sod of the new line was cut in May, 1880 by Mrs Fell junior, and the first train ran on New Year's Day, 1881. An impressive track record! The line was of three foot gauge, roughly 6½ miles long, and cost £15,000, which was somewhat more than the estimate.

The system used by Fell ignored the usual method of embankment and cutting to achieve a level trackbed, and instead relied on viaducts to carry the line. Prefabricated frames were adapted to the varying ground levels. He first patented the system in 1873, and later in 1879 an improved scheme with additional strengthening timbers, was also patented.

The Marland railway crossed at least five viaducts, as opposed to bridges, but the most eye-catching and by far the longest was the first, taking the little railway across the river Torridge and its wide valley. Its overall length was more than 300 yards and at one point travellers found themselves perched 40 feet above the ground. The main section consisted of five spans crossing the river, the largest three being 45 feet each, and the flanking spans 18 feet. These piers were supported on brick bases and brick cutwaters in the river. Four more spans connected the viaduct to the solid ground and the loop line immediately before the tunnel under the road leading to the station. There were 42 spans in all, and amazingly most of the simple timber piers had no proper foundations.

It was a truly remarkable feat of engineering and it drew much comment and attention. Mr Fell had intended it as something of a showpiece, and it is recorded that not only did the War Office inspect the line and express interest in its novel design, but a considerable stir was caused when the secretary of the Chinese Legation travelled down to look at this highly practical railway, with a view to using similar constructions in his own country.

This report of the opening of the line and the first passenger train comes from the Bideford Gazette.

"At 12 o'clock precisely the whistle blew, and the small party were taken at once gently through a short tunnel, some of them raising a faint cheer. On emerging, however, and getting on to the slender-looking bridge, right above the river Torridge, and from thence on to a timber viaduct, 266 yards in length, and forty feet in height, the feeling of jollity suddenly changed to one of wonder and tremulation – wonder that engineering skill could devise so light a structure combined with safety, and tremulation lest the one thought upper-most in the minds of all should be realised. A looker-on from the common above afterwards informed us that the movement of the

train across the viaduct as he looked down upon it presented the appearance of a party of children being conveyed across a toy bridge in perambulators. Even the lazy cattle which had been before quietly grazing in the meadow by the river were startled at this new intrusion upon their quietude, and went frisking along in all sorts of attitudes to seek shelter in the hedge beyond. As however, steam was put on, and we rattled along on what was, comparatively speaking, terra firma, around the thickly wooded slopes of Penclive (sic) Valley, reassurance returned, only to leave us again on finding ourselves on a viaduct crossing a narrow gorge dividing a most picturesque and well studded wood. In fact the scenery through which the line passes from beginning to end is of such a character as can rarely be seen from any railway in England. Over viaducts (ten in number) with perfectly upright supports, through the centre of woods, up steep gradients, over boggy moors, then falling on a sharp gradient of one in thirty, all the while making some pretty sharp curves, and all of this on a line not 6½ miles in length is a kind of travelling such as Devonshire people are unaccustomed to in their own county. It was possibly this fact that struck terror to the hearts of some of the more innocent and less experienced of the party but by-and-by noticing that Mr Fell himself was at the front, and that the engine was under the complete control of the driver, noticing also that on each viaduct there was a substantial guard rail, and then recollecting, too that Mont Cenis had been conquered by this same skilful engineer with his light railway, all qualms died away, and the return journey, found us devoting more attention to the scenery above and below than to the distance we were from mother earth, and discussing the probabilities of extending this most useful piece of railway on to Hatherleigh, and from there on to Sampford Courtenay, there joining the Okehampton line."

"The first experiences of travelling over a light railway may be unpleasant, but everyone saw that the element of complete safety was combined with the lightness and the cheapness of a railway of this kind."

Who knows how many countries subsequently employed Fell's ideas — perhaps there are still a few Fell viaducts in use in remote corners of the globe?

By 1912 the state of the timbers was causing some concern and it was noted that the Torridge viaduct was in need of some repair. An iron girder replaced the span over the road in 1913, but the remainder had to wait until long after the end of the Grear War, which effectively halted the clay works, and any maintenance on the line, which was lucky to survive at all.

The timber used was 8"x4" for the main verticals and 4"x3" for the remainder. Over the years supports and cross bracings were used to strengthen the weakening timbers — but it was not until the early years of this century that major repair work was undertaken. Modern motorways do not last as long. And it is interesting that the condition of the replacement structure is such that even walkers are not allowed to cross until vital repairs have been carried out.

To spread the load on his seemingly flimsly structures, Fell commissioned special engines with a nine foot long wheel base. The public at first were wary, but as soon as it was apparent that no collapse was going to occur, considerable use was made of the little clay train.

Initially only workmen used the line, apart from the clay that is, but in 1909 two redundant horse tramcars were purchased from London County Council, and these were converted for passenger use on the line. It is not thought that they have survived, ending their lives as foremen's huts at the clayworks.

Many suggestions had been put forward for a railway linking Hatherleigh with Torrington, or with Okehampton. It was a busy market town and felt its isolation from the rail network. But World War I interrupted all plans, and it was not until 30th June, 1922 that the first sod of the North Devon & Cornwall Junction Light Railway was cut — at Halwill Junction. It had become something of a government project to benefit the unemployed — somewhat like road-building and landowner's schemes after the Napoleonic wars. It had been agreed that construction workers and wagons would make use of the Marland line, but without detriment to the clay trade, much reduced as a result of the War. The viaducts had to be strengthened and there were continual wrangles over the state of the line — was it rotten anyway or had the contractors damaged it with overloading? One problem was the Torridge viaduct — which Col H Stephens, the promoter and builder of the NDCJLR, which was to be standard gauge – realised would not take even the extra wieght of a standard gauge wagon, let alone an engine.

The Marland railway was eventually sold to the NDCJLR for £18,000, and the line opened in July, 1925. But before this date, the old timber viaduct had been replaced, with the utilitarian concrete and iron structure that we see today.

The branch line finally connected North Devon with South, and gave passengers some interesting choices. Exeter could be reached either via Halwill Junction and Okehampton, or via Bideford and Barnstaple. Bude and Cornwall were also within reach, as were the main line stations at Exeter and Plymouth from either the up or down platforms. Halwill Junction in its heyday was the Clapham of Devon.

But traffic was dwindling; the roads were also improved, and with the advent of British Rail it was only a question of time. In 1964 all goods traffic except milk and clay were halted on the line. And on 1st March, 1965, the passenger service was withdrawn.

The line finally closed in August, 1982. Today much of the Barnstaple to Marland line is part of a long distance footpath, the Tarka Trail – and the clay is transported by road.

Yelland Electricity Power Station

A Bideford Gazette reporter was attracted by the myriad lights and night-time activity. He drove down to have a look and gave us this report ....

"the huge main structure looms up fantastically. A fussy light engine hissed across the rail track. Ahead were the concrete studs in the river bed, preparation for the new T shaped jetty for the coal-carrying ships. Passing rows of brightly lit offices, one could peep from a wooden platform down 60 feet to where excavations are being made for the concrete chamber. This being below the lowest part of the river bed cuts into the remnants of prehistoric times.

The scene is into something of the fantasy of a Jules Verne creation yet all the time the great project persists and soon these marsh meadows will be covered by a manmade scientific marvel."

That was in April. By October considerable progress had been made, as a more prosaic account reported. Of the two chimneys, one was complete, having reached to 120 feet — a low level, apparently, for power station chimneys, because of Chivenor across the estuary. The jetty, when finished, would be 530 feet in length and was fast approaching completion. Deep underground excavations were proceeding to drive the circulating water intake tunnel out into the river whilst on the site of the works the water discharge channel was being excavated. About one sixth of the main building superstructure was complete, sufficient to house one turbo generator and two boilers, then being erected, and work was proceeding on the construction of the foundations for the second and third turbo-alternators which would complete the first half of the station.

Considering the size of the project, there was very little fuss about its completion — and absolutely no ceremony. From the contemporary newspaper report it seems that they discovered Yelland was operational almost by accident. This may have been because it was gradually phased in over a period of two years. The first generator began supplying the national grid on 1st August, 1953 — with 400 amp, and 100 amps going to Roundswell. As the

half of the turbine room shows two generate
was taken the one at the rear was only n

FIRST STAGE OF TRANSIT FROM SHIP TO SHORE

At the heart of the East Yelland Power Station stands the main control room pictured above. Eventually ea k panels in the foreground will be connected to and will control one of the six generators which will be accom the completed station. In the background are the control panels and switches for generators, feeders and grid lin iad of gauges to show the output of the station and the way in which it is linked up, at any particular momer system.

(Stuart J. Turner, Bide ave been commissioned, alth Boilers Nos. 5 and 6 for the t

coal jetty was not complete, all the fuel had to come by road, and there was some difficulty in keeping up with the 15-20 tons per hour needed.

By the middle of October the system improved with the completion of the jetty and the first coal boat was unloaded, the fuel being carried by conveyor belt to the boiler house.

By 1980 its future was in doubt. The station was then 30 years old and generating methods had progressed. It was old, and old-fashioned. In 1982 the Journal Herald reported that the CEGB were looking for a new site for a new station in the Westcountry, and mentioned Yelland as a possibility. At that time it was employing 140 people, and its three 3-megawatt generators supplied enough power for 90,000 one-bar electric fires! By this time it was only used to top up the national grid at times of peak demand, but during the December storms of 1981 it provided power to North Devon when outside supplies failed.

The report added that it had cost £12 million to build, and was to be replaced by a £2 million sub-station at Alverdiscott.

The end came on 4th July, 1987. The twin chimneys, now 230 feet in height (unless this is a typographical error), had charges of 25lb laid against them. And at 12 noon precisely, according to the report, they were detonated by a student, and gently collapsed. The event attracted very little attention, and local people soon got used to an estuary view without the chimneys and the utilitarian block. After all, it had only been there for just over thirty years, and that, in the span of the estuary, is but a passing moment. It would have been nice if the CEGB could have left the site as they found it — marshland and riverbank, in keeping with and continuing the neighbouring lands. But the site was sold to Daniel Homes, London developers. They were faced with the prospect of demolishing the power station itself, with its 500 tons of dangerous asbestos lagging.

There has been talk of proposed marina and a time-share village — incorporating "leisure facilities" as a sop to the natives — as if wandering along unspoilt riverbank was not leisure facility enough — so there seems little chance of Yelland every returning to its pre CEGB state. Nationalised interests seem not to be very good at safeguarding the nation's natural resources.

A distant view of Instow looks, at first glance, as if it has altered very little since the early years of this century. But a closer inspection shows that the waterfront site once occupied by the *Marine Hotel* is now occupied by a similarly tall block of flats. And the private house behind, known as Strandfield and obscured by trees, has grown and, grown, into the Commodore Hotel.

The Marine Hotel was a very old building, although never considered sufficiently important to list. Belived to date from the mid 18th century, it was included in the purchase by Commodore Clevland of the Tapeley Estate from the Giffords. Apparently the hotel had been built on the site of the former Instow manor house. Presumably it jogged along comfortably as a summer lodging for visitors who journeyed as far as remote North Devon, and probably made a living out of families who came, not for one or two weeks, but for two or more months. All this changed when the railway reached Instow in 1856.

The year before the Marine had changed hands, and the following advertisement appeared in the North Devon Journal.

"Thomas Parramore, late of the New Inn, Bideford, begs to inform the Nobility, Gentry and Commercials that he is now at the above inn and has fitted it up with every domestic comfort and convenience.

The house contains excellent Sitting Rooms and Bed Rooms all looking into the River Torridge and also impressive delightful views of the Atlantic, Lundy Island, Bar and Light House. The succession of Sailing Ships and Steamers constantly on the river, with Fishing and Yachting, and its contiguity to the North Devon Railway and Cricket Ground, makes it one of the most delectable Residences in England.

The Proprietor also begs to inform Gentlemen who delight in FIELD SPORTS that he has succeeded in obtaining the Right of shooting over some Thousand Acres of the far-famed Braunton Burrows and also trout Fishing in the neighbourhood."

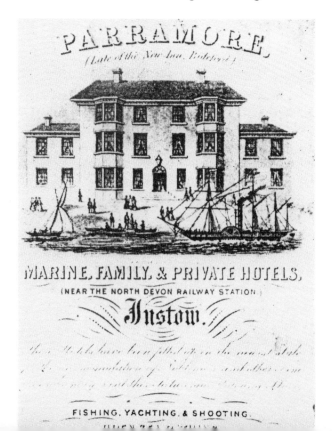

Choice wines and Spirits, Good Stabling, and a Lock-up Coach House were also part of the manifold attractions, and at the very bottom of the notice is a line:

"TP also begs to announce that he has taken the Commercial Hotel at Bideford."

The next report is not so advantageous to Mr Parramore — a providence-sent name for a hotelier if ever there was one, and the Marine was speedily renamed "Parramore's Hotel". Later that same year two of his guests, having spent most of the day on the water and being "pretty well liquored up" decided on a spot of shooting practice from the hotel windows. Unfortunately they chose a sailing boat out on the sands — and even more unfortunately, Sam Fishley and his son were on board. The lad was hit, but not seriously, and the report concludes with the recommendation that the two young men would do better to offer themselves to the General in charge at Sebastapol where they might find all the shooting they could wish for.

Mr Parramore had bought the lease of the hotel from a Mr J Moggridge, and he had obviously spent no little effort and money in bringing it up to date. Perhaps that was how he operated, or perhaps it was not as profitable as he had hoped. Whatever the reason, a four day sale in October, 1857, was held to dispose of the entire contents, from oil paintings to kitchen goods, clothing, and the horses and carriages — and several hundred yards of oil cloth. The reason given was that the premises had been let as a whole to a private family.

But in 1859 a licence was granted to William Winch for the Marine Hotel — its old name back again. (Mr Parramore continued to operate at what is now Tanton's, transferring the name Parramore's hotel from the Marine).

The original building was added to over the years, until finally it occupied almost the entire area between the sea wall and the road. The Christie Estate, descendants of Commodore Clevland, took stock of their ageing possession in 1968, and had a surveyors report prepared. The hotel had 30 bedrooms and 8 bathrooms. The heating and hot water was supplied by two solid fuel boilers,

which gave problems, and much of the kitchen equipment was found to be out of date and a handicap to the staff. In short, the Marine "was becoming inadequate by modern standards."

The hotel closed in December, 1971, and the estate put the property up for sale. Various local hoteliers showed considerable interest. It was the only large hotel in Instow — the Commodore did not then exist — and one of North Devon's premier hotels. It was eventually sold for around £110,000 to R Harris & sons, of Barnstaple, who at that time were part of the Courtline shipping and holiday group, and the assumption was that it would continue to be run as a hotel. Events proved otherwise, and in June, 1974, the old Marine was demolished.

With **Durrant House Hotel** it is more a case of being buried rather than vanished! The square, stuccoed 19th century house must have been a familiar sight to travellers between Bideford and Northam. At one time it was the home of Sir Richard Keats who retired there in 1816 after a long and distinguished naval career in which he saw action with both Nelson and Wellington. He died in 1834.

This view of the Durrant House Hotel, proprietor Miss C Halstead, comes from an early Bideford guide book, where it is referred to as a 'gracious Georgian mansion standing in three acres of delightful grounds.'

Since then the hotel has grown — and grown — and grown. But somewhere at its heart there still stands the old original.

A similar process has happened at both the Commodore Hotel, Instow, once a house called Strandfield, and at the Saunton Sands Hotel across the Bay, where the original house can be clearly seen from the road.

Bideford Quay as we know it today was about the last improvement to be carried out to the town; almost everything that has been done since is questionable, and an improvement only in the eyes of the perpetrators.

The old Quay stopped short at today's Post Office. Here the Pill river ran inland to become the Kenwith stream, crossed by an ancient causeway which formed the only link with Northam and Appledore.

In 1825 work began on embanking, and thus draining, the low-lying and marshy ground to the north of the Pill. This formed the area of land that became Victoria Park and, more importantly, the causeway that became known as the River Bank. It was not until 1844 that the connecting bridge was built, thus linking the embankment with the Quay, and enabling a footpath to be created between Bideford and Northam and Appledore.

As the town expanded and became more prosperous, so the ideas of its worthy Aldermen and councillors grew. After the last widening of the Quay proper in 1890, it was decided to include the River Bank. A promenade was built beyond the Pill, and trees planted all the way along its length from the Bridge northwards. That was in 1891.

How sad that the centenary of this should be commemorated by the council of the day consenting to the destruction of that same avenue. Some of the trees may have died and been replaced over the years, but the continuity had always been preserved.

Not now.

Large bare gaps.

All to make way for a car park. How the worthy aldermen must have turned in their graves.

The Promenade Bideford

"*A beautiful avenue of trees*"

KINGSLEY STATUE AND ARMADA GUNS BIDEFORD

From an early guidebook ....

"Many acres of marsh land were purchased by the town and gradually laid out with the result that there is a large open space for sports encircled by a cycle track, the whole being bounded by a most pleasant riverside walk, plentifully provided with seats, placed under a beautiful avenue of trees. The view from this walk is a magnificent one, embracing the river and surrounding hills down as far as Instow, whilst on the other hand is the ancient bridge ...."

RIP

Barnstaple

One of the tragedies of the twentieth century and its way of life is the destruction of our towns. They are still there, geographically speaking, and they are still busy. But the reasons for their existence have gone, and with them, their dignity. Towns today are merely shopping centres, merry-go-rounds of commerce and places where people live in huddles, all totally interdependent. Yet each town sprang up for a specific purpose, for a good reason. And it was this reason that attracted the people to live, and to carry on their businesses. Barnstaple grew around the lowest fordable, or bridgeable, point of the River Taw. It was a meeting place for those waiting to cross in safety before the building of the first bridge, and out of this grew its status as a market town. The river also brought prominence as a sea port, serving much of North Devon and Somerset. It was natural that it should become the major commercial centre, the administrative centre, and the largest centre of population.

The new link road has by-passed the old town on the southern side although this now stretches out to embrace its link with the motorway system and, it thinks, untold gold. A proposed downstream bridge will by-pass it on the northern side, and the venerable old stone structure which has seen such centuries of service will be used only by local traffic and pedestrians. The port closed early this century and only a handful of local sandbarges now tie up alongside the revamped and glamourised quay. Where once all was bustle and business, noisy with sailors and fishermen, untidy with the clutter of loading and unloading, all is now neat and architect-award-winning-designed. There is no whiff of fish, no sign of nets, no broad Devonian curses. Only no-parking notices and brightly painted bollards which would shrink in horror at the thought of having nasty tarry ropes wrapped round them. The railway station that was so conveniently close to hand is now a restaurant, only the old signal box remaining, full of railway memorabilia. The lines ran along the quay, crossing the river on a curving iron bridge to link up with the branch line to Exeter. The line closed in October, 1970, and the bridge was demolished in 1977.

The Lynton train approaches across the Taw Bridge.

Almost gone   1977

THE OLD DRAWBRIDGE, BARNSTAPLE.

It could be said that Barnstaple Quay as generations of Barumites knew it, is itself a vanished landmark.

An important feature was the old swing bridge that took the railway line to Lynton across the waters of the Yeo. This finally clanged shut in October, 1970, and the last time the bridge opened was the next January to allow a large cabin cruiser through.

Higher up the Yeo was another interesting bridge. To allow shipping through to the wharves that once lined the banks, a second swing bridge carried the Braunton road across the creek. It was built in 1829 by W Gould of Barnstaple, replaced with a more sturdy-looking structure that continued in use until it was removed in October 1978.

A very early print of Rolle Quay . . .

Rolle Quay, too, has changed out of all recognition. The same tidying up, the same shift away from its original purpose to become another business street with some newly conceived housing — and a neat protective wall in case any of the parked cars should decide to take the plunge into the muddy inlet that was once such a busy shipping channel.

The buildings fronting Rolle Quay would have been the usual jumble of sheds and warehouses, cottages and pubs and chandlers, all long since gone or altered beyond recognition. But the one building that survived until 1983 was the imposing Victoria Flour Mill. It was a magnificent example of Victorian industrial architecture and the council was correct in its first refusal for permission to demolish when it stated that the building was too important. It takes a special kind of eye and a sympathetic governing body to see the possibilities of these relics of a bygone age. A second application was successful. So down it came, cast iron pillars, hoists and cranes — and up went the predictable blocks of flats, so glibly

. . . the swing bridge can just be seen

considered to be 'in keeping', but in reality reproduced all over the country in all kinds of settings, and in keeping with nothing in particular except the last decades of the twentieth century.

Victoria Flour Mill was built in 1899 and was considered to be one of the most up-to-date modern flour mills in the county. A steam engine of 120 horse power drove the steel roller-grinders, capable of turning out six sacks of flour per hour, and at its peak the mill must have been very busy as it is recorded Rolle Quay handled 100,000 tons of goods in one year. A mobile crane mounted on rails was the last reminder of this busy past, used to unload the ships that came from all along the Channel coasts, and from further afield. Now that last little piece of history has gone, the rails covered by a layer of ubiquitous tarmac.

The mill stopped grinding some time in the 1920's and the building was bought by Trumps in 1933, who used it largely for storing flour, grain and cattle feed, brought across from their South Wales mills. Its death knell was sounded when on 27th

February, 1966, it caught fire. The flames were spotted, late at night, and it took the combined efforts of six fire brigades to bring the fire under control. The adjoining premises were badly damaged and the Victoria Flour Mill itself was left a shell. But it was repaired and continued in use for many years.

The first application in 1981 was turned down, but in the end the planners gave way and another piece of Barnstaple's heritage vanished.

The railway bridge across the Yeo

The *Castle House,* Barnstaple was demolished early in June, 1976. The site was levelled and grassed, and many people have forgotten that it ever existed. Only the lodge house and gates remain.

Architecturally speaking, this is no great loss. It was just another amorphous Victorian pile, no doubt a rabbit warren of corridors and staircases that ended its days as inconvenient and overcrowded Borough Council offices.

The site was an ancient one. At one time the whole area would have been included in the curtilage of the Norman castle. There would have been kitchens, storerooms, barracks, stables, and all the bustle associated with a castle stronghold. The Castle House itself is shown on a map of 1770, and it was thought to occupy the site of the old castle chantry, possibly using salvaged stone, and must have been a most interesting and historic property.

It was in the ownership of the Chichester family, and in April, 1860 the freehold was offered for sale in two lots. The Navie Yard was purchased by the tenant, James Oliver, for £630, and Lot 1, the Castle House, was sold to James Gay Hiern for £1,700. It was, however, subject to the "life interest of a lady aged 74, on whose decease the property falls in hand".

Did Mr Hiern have long to wait? Certainly by early 1865 he was in possession. A report presented by Miss F Hunt (a daughter of the Mayor of Barnstaple) relates the grisly discovery of human skeletons underneath the Castle House.

"late in the occupation of Sir Wm. Rac, KCB, and now the property of Hiern esq. The property was undergoing considerable alterations. An old Boundary wall was taken down and a new one built. Also a wing of the house was demolished and underneath was a kind of cellar which did not extend more than two feet beneath the surface of the ground."

Miss Hunt went to examine this excavation and found men building a new cellar to a further depth of seven or eight feet. They had come on a:

"deposit of human bones, in one case there were four sculls or portions in immediate proximity to each other. Altogether they counted 18, which number they were most positive was correct. To all appearances they had been most hastily interred as the remains were much contorted. In one of the sculls the teeth were perfect in the lower jaw. Col H carried one of them away. The skeletons are supposed by him to have belonged to 17 men who were hung then, at the assizes in 15-- which were held here, as the plague raged at Exeter."

An earlier report from the same lady seems to indicate that Mr Hiern let the Castle House – and the tenants were somewhat troubled by strange noises.

"Captain White having left 'Gorwell' went to live at Castle House. During his residence, the household were often much dis-turbed by noises in the lower part of the house which they at first attributed to rats.

After a diligent search however, this was found not to be the case. The noises continued. On some occasions when the whole household were aroused Captain White, armed with a stick, would march at the head of his family and search the house, but invariably traced the noises to the scullery under a wing of the house.

"Residence of W P Hiern, built on the site of old Castle, walls of which are incorporated"

As the Borough Offices.

One one occasion, the family being absent, dining out, the servants were much alarmed by hearing more noises also in the scullery. At last some of them left and the rest slept there in a room away from the said wing.

Capt White soon died after and the house was left empty. Sir Wm Rac was there for a short time but he had the wing shut off.

These facts were communicated to me by Ann Hartnole, who, during the time in question lived with Capt White. She testified to the great annoyance caused by the noises but avers that none of the servants know of the fact of criminals having been buried under the said scullery."

An even earlier account relates how William Wavell, MD, carried out improvements in 1790 and discovered a skeleton in a vault under the wine cellar which was "not disturbed."

In 1890 the old house disappeared completely and in its place a grand new house, castellated, towered and turretted, was built for Mr W P Hiern. This was designed by Mr W C Oliver, father of Bruce Oliver, who later became a well known borough councillor and local historian, and partner in the firm of Oliver & Dyer. Mr Hiern was a reknowned botanist who classified and catalogued the botanical section of the British Museum and Library. A huge conservatory was a prominent feature, and the grounds were beautifully laid out with trees and shrubs. Later photographs show the walls covered with creepers and climbers.

At this time the grounds were surrounded by high walls, so that neither castle nor house could be seen, although Mr Hiern did throw open the grounds for fetes etc.

In 1926, Barnstaple Borough Council decided to purchase the house and grounds for the sum of £4,600. The house became the council offices, and what was once Mr Hiern's beautifully laid out garden became a plain grassed area devoid of anything except some paths – and one tree reduced to an unsightly and pathetic stump in 1964.

It was bursting at the seams when reorganisation in 1974 forced the council to consider new premises. The tall tower block across the road went up – and in 1976 the Castle House came down. There are some who consider the new even more unsightly than the old but as an office building it is undoubtedly more efficient.

This aerial view shows Castle House and Dornats factory, and much else besides that has gone.

The Old Bridewell building in Tooley Street, Barnstaple, is better known to most of us as the site of **Dornats** bottling factory, Tuly Street. Over 300 years old, it was built as a merchant's warehouse, before becoming the town's bridewell, or poor house, and it was superseded by the union workhouse in Alexandra Road, built in 1831. The building became, briefly, a wool combing factory, then a brewery.

Charles Camille Dornat was a French wine expert, a chemist and an apothecary. He left France in 1840 for this country, and by 1861 had established himself in business in Holland Street. In 1870 he moved to the Old Bridewell, and his business thrived.

In 1934 up-to-date machinery was installed which was the very last word in the scientific production of mineral water. By this time the proprietors were the Youing family, descendants of Dornats.

In 1950, Dornats was one of the oldest surviving soft drinks manufacturers in the country. They produced lemonade, ginger ale, mineral water and other cordials, but they also bottled extensively for Guinness, Bass, Watneys and other major brewing firms, who in those days transported their beers and stouts in bulk, relying on local wholesalers or bottling plants to bottle their elixirs.

During the War Dornats helped the war effort by bottling Pepsi-Cola for the American troops, who would undoubtedly have gone into decline without their national beverage.

The mineral water company closed in 1980, and the building was sold to a developer. It was referred to as "the old lemonade factory" and had been bought with the possibility of it becoming an ice rink and entertainment centre. However, despite being a listed building, it was decided the ancient structure was beyond repair, and demolition was allowed to take place.

St Mary's Magdelene

In the days when everyone went to church on Sunday and worshipped at the House of God instead of the house of commerce, Barnstaple found itself in need of several new churches to serve the fast expanding town. It was unthinkable that the citizens, however poor, should be deprived of their spiritual solace and instruction, and the Aldermen and councillors saw it as their duty to ensure that no-one had an excuse not to attend, and that everyone had a church within walking distance. The splendid buildings and tall spires that represented the church architecture of the day were an inspiration and a symbol of hope in lives of poverty and drabness; nowadays they build supermarkets instead.

One of the problems was that the existing parish church of St Peter and St Paul was not only full to overflowing, but the system of pew rental barred most of the poorer folk from attending. Although the system was decried by many, it raised much needed money for the church and was difficult to overturn without offending the wealthier parishioners. A new church was seen as the

75

answer, especially since the town was fast expanding.

The story of St Mary Magdalene, or Maudlin, is interesting in that it provided a link with the past, continuity with the town's ecclesiastical history, which is now completely lost.

Contemporary with the building of Barnstaple's Norman castle was the founding of a priory dedicated to St Mary Magdalene. The same man, Judhael of Totnes, was responsible for both, and the priory was of the Cluniac order, the foundation being recorded in 1107. It occupied a site outside the town walls, stretching from the north gate to the east gate and bounded by the river Yeo and the road now known as Vicarage Street. The suppression of the monasteries came under Henry VIII and on 4th February, 1536, the monks left their home and church for ever and handed the keys to the King's commissioners.

The buildings stood empty, and no doubt the process of decay and stone robbing quickly set in. Then in 1538 Lord William Howard, son of the second Duke of Norfolk, was granted the priory and lands. He later became Lord Howard of Effingham, and there is no record of him developing, or showing much interest in, the priory itself. His main concern was with the trading rights and jurisdiction of his lands, and he was in dispute with the town on more than one occasion.

The Howards sold in 1613, and again in 1699 two portions of the "site and ruins of the demolished priory house and gardens called St Mary Magdalene alias Maudlin" were sold to two Barnstaple men.

It seems that part of the priory buildings was sufficiently sound to be turned into a house, or lodging for distinguished visitors, and was known as Maudlyn Rack Close. This was last mentioned in 1707. There seems little trace today of that ancient foundation which must once have been a major influence on the town. Remnants of walling were discovered in a house at the entrance to Coronation Street and revealed a building some 88 feet long and 32 feet wide, with eight bays divided by shallow buttresses, and part of an original doorway in the north side. It may well have been a storehouse, but it is thought that the main priory buildings occupied the area known as Rackfields.

The foundation stone of the new St Mary Magdalene church

was laid on 23rd October, 1844, by the Archdeacon of Barnstaple — but not without some intrigues and devious manipulation first. The Rev Scott, then curate at Pilton, stepped in with the generous offer of £2,000 for the proposed new church. He and Mr Abbott of Bideford were two of the keenest supporters and a site was found for the church at Lady Meadow. It transpired that Mr Abbott was to be the architect — and that the Rev Scott was himself to be the first vicar, and wanted to reserve the living for himself and his nominees. So keen were these two gentlemen that they began work without the full agreement of the committee or of the church building societies, both of whom vetoed the proposals on the grounds of site, and the church designs proving too expensive. The Rev Scott withdrew himself and his offer and the committee started again. (The Rev Scott reappears as the builder of Holy Trinity church at Newport — at his own expense and, yes, he was the first incumbent).

A new site was found in the Rack Park area, and it was coincidental that it was only about 250 yards from the site of the ancient priory, and that Higher and Lower Maudlin streets (named after the priory) were at the north end. The architect this time was to be Benjamin Ferry, a pupil of Pugin and vice-president of the RIBA.

It seems the Rev Scott was determined to have his revenge, for Holy Trinity was consecrated in June, 1845, but without its spire, and something of a race developed between the two churches as to which should be completed first. In the event St Mary's Magdalene was "topped off" first, amidst much rejoicing. The final cost was £4,363, including £500 for the site, and the consecration service took place on 10th November, 1846. Holy Trinity had cost £6,000 — and the site had been given. It appears only to have lasted twenty years before we learn of Gilbert rebuilding it, only the tower from the original remaining.

A full description of the church comes from the Reverend R J E Boggis' book on the parish and church of St Mary Magdalene, of which he was vicar.

"The church is a really beautiful and well-proportioned edifice of transitional Early English style, and is an unusually favourable example of its time. It consists of a sanctuary, a choir

flanked by side chapels, a nave and aisles with arcades of five arches, and a south porch with tower and spire above it. There is a doorway at the west end of the nave, and another in the north aisle, opposite the south porch, and a small clergy vestry north of the sanctuary. All these belong to the original fabric, and there is also a choir vestry of recent date, adjoining the north wall of the north chapel. The dimensions of the building are these: – exterior length 122 feet, interior length 111 feet, exterior breadth (including porch and choir vestry) 89 feet, interior breadth 48 feet, height of nave (from floor to apex of roof) 35 feet, height of tower and spire (to the top of the vane) 120 feet.

The sum of money available for the building and the furnishing of the church was very small in amount and consequently the fittings had to be of the cheapest description, as – most wisely and most fortunately – the fabric was thoroughly good and well constructed, except that the outside walls had much perishable stone incorporated in them. One result of the scarcity of funds was that the church was paved with flags of a sort of grey limestone, and under the wooden flooring was left a vacant space. The flag-stones were dull in appearance, and "sweated" profusely in damp weather, while, owing to imperfect ventilation, dry rot was working havoc with the joists and boards; so the first care of the Church Improvement Scheme Committee of 1908 was to fill in the space beneath the floor (except at the west end), and to set on concrete beds red tiling in the alleys and red deal blocks for the flooring.

The seating consists of fixed benches of deal, stained a dark colour, and the seats for the choir are of the same cheap material. Originally the church was said to have 802 sittings, but now, the pews having been set at a more convenient distance from each other, there is comfortable accommodation for only about 550. Red hassocks were supplied in 1910, the cost (£18) being covered by the sale of a book entitled Hints for the Home, which was edited by Mrs Boggis; and about the same time the pews were provided by the expenditure of £31 with red and black felt carpet-seating from the warehouse of Mr F. Kempe of Barnstaple. The stalls for the clergy, made to match the other wood-work, were given by the Reverend A.W.L. Rivett. Originally there were two parclose screens, stained the same colour as the seats; but in 1884 these were removed from the archways on either side of the choir, and set in the openings between the chapels and the aisles. The timber of the roof, which is an open one of beautiful design, is of chestnut.

The pulpit and the font (the latter being the gift of the Reverend Dr R. Hayne, Vicar of Pilton) are of Caen stone, the one being octagonal in shape and raised six steps above the floor of the church, and the other round and set on one step. Originally the font fittingly occupied a central position near the west end of the nave, but it was shifted to a place near the south door in 1899. Its flat cover of oak, mounted in iron, was given by Mr Percy Windsor and Mr William Bryant in 1898; the oak ewer, bound with brass, was presented in 1903 by Mrs Emma Sanders; and the baptismal shell of mother-of-pearl and silver was provided by Mrs Shephard in 1904."

"The sanctuary is adorned with two coloured windows. The five-light east window, which is coæval with the church – it was a poor time for stained glass, but this is not obtrusively bad – has in the bottom row the Madonna with the Holy Child and the four Major Prophets; in the middle five scenes from the life of St Mary Magdalene (her cure, her ministering to the Lord, the Crucifixion, her arrival at the tomb, and her meeting the risen Saviour); in the row above, the Ascension and the four Evangelists; and in the top tracery the pelican in her piety, the Agnus Dei, and the coats-of-arms of the United Kingdom and of the Archdiocese of Canterbury and of the Diocese of Exeter. For this window and its fixing Mr Charles Hudson was paid the surprisingly small sum of £78-8-3, more than half of which came from the Luxmoore family. The south window, which happily is seen by few persons, has gaudily coloured portraits of King Solomon at the building and at the dedication of the Temple, inserted in 1855 to commemorate Mr John Thomas Britton, who was a Freemason."

"The well-proportioned but diminutive south chapel was long used as an organ-chamber and place for the singers. Here was set the seraphim, which used to accompany the singing in the early years of the church, and which was succeeded in 1867 by a small pipe-organ from Exeter – remarkable for having the usual arrangement of white and black notes reversed. Then, when the new organ was placed on the other side and the choir were robed, this chapel

was converted into a choir vestry. Later it served as a sort of lumber-room, until on January 18th, 1914, it was dedicated as a Lady Chapel, the cost of the work, amounting to £100, being given or collected by the Vicar.

The Reverend Boggis has left a faithful record of his life and that of St. Mary's during his ministry in the form of two scrap books. These are full of church notices, the services held, the hymns appointed, church outings, and all the minor events that go to make up the full pattern of a busy parish. Sadly it was not continued after he retired in 1918, but he appears to have entered fully into local life and instigated many events — such as a Smoking Concert held in the mission hall in 1908 — men only! He also left a description of his predecessors at St Mary's, given as part of his last sermon.

The first vicar, James Pycroft resigned the living "in order that he might indulge his predilection for literature and for cricket" after ten years service. Henry Bull gave 27 years service before moving to the country parish of Roborough. The next incumbent (John Gewkie) stayed only two years before deciding to devote his time to the study of the Bible. Alfred William Lovely Rivett went "to escape the serious difficulties and disappointments he had experienced" after 12 years. Edward Windsor, retired honourably after 10 years, which brings us to 1907, and the Reverend Boggis.

In 1884 a new organ was built in the north chapel, and singing became an important part of the church's life.

An interesting addition came in 1912 when the church bought for £32 10s the former chapel-of-ease from Mortehoe. This was used as a church hall.

The church was particularly proud of its avenue of lime trees planted along the south approach and of the many ornamental shrubs in the churchyard. This ceased to be used for interments after 1903, but boasted two centenarians amongst the graves.

The original boundaries of the new parish were drawn in such a way that the mother parish of St Peter retained all the better class houses, streets and shops, assigning only the slum and pauper areas to St Mary's. This was later amended, after much fighting, and Ebberley Lawn, Fort Street and Terrace, Alexandra Road, Bear

Street and some of Boutport Street were passed over.

By 1976 talk of amalgamation and a team ministry was in the air. Falling congregations in the two town churches caused concern at Diocesan level, and as it was unthinkable that the historic parish church should close, it was the firmly held view of many of the ex-parishioners of St Mary's, that St Mary-Mags drew the short straw. Their last vicar, appointed in 1976, became the first minister in charge of the combined parishes, and in October 1977, St Mary Magdalene was declared redundant, and closed.

A structural report in 1978 drew attention to serious faults in the structure, and the church was considered unsafe. It was demolished, and the site sold for housing. The name remains, as it always has, linking the new with the ancient. At the entrance to the flats are the church wall and gateway, and to the rear the avenue of lime trees lead through the now deserted churchyard, with the headstones lining the walls. It has about it still the air of peace associated with God's Acre, and is for ever a green and tranquil oasis amidst the roar of the town.

Built originally as the Union workhouse under the new Poor Laws, the *Alexandra Hospital* became in turn a maternity hospital and latterly a home for the elderly. It was constructed in 1831 at a cost of £4,000, and in 1850 it was recorded as housing 220 paupers.

The building had been boarded up since 1978 and was sold at auction in 1982, and demolished to make way for housing.

The chapel, which was built later in 1855, still stands – a condition of the planning permission being that it be retained for community use.

FOR AUCTION: Barnstaple's Alexandra Hospital, empty for four years, goes under the hammer next month for demolition. The site, covering nearly two acres, is scheduled for residential development

The North Devon Infirmary ended its days hopelessly over-crowded, hopelessly out of date — hopelessly inadequate to cope with the growing needs of the area and demands of modern medicine. Yet in its day it was a remarkable example of what could be provided by the nineteenth century ethic of self-help.

It was opened in 1826, built entirely by public subscription, and ran entirely on public subscription. There was no National Health to foot the bill. Yet the NDI served everyone, rich and poor alike, and not until 1921 was it decided to request the wealthier patients to contribute towards their maintenance.

Medical staff had to be tough in those days. The building was three storeys high, but there was no lift until the 1880's. The water supply came from cisterns filled from wells — baths were an unheard of luxury. Not until 1859 was a proper water supply connected.

A new operating theatre was provided in 1882 by Dr Richard Budd, physician to the NDI for nearly 40 years. And in 1921, 'a costly and up to date electric lift' replaced the earlier lift — presumably hand operated. The X-ray department came in 1924.

Shortage of funds is nothing new, for we read in the centenary booklet that a maternity ward was proposed, and that this could occupy the Bassett ward, closed in March, 1911, because of lack of funds.

In its centenary year, 1926, the Board decided to attempt to raise £10,000 for building projects. A special open air service was held in Rock Park in August of that year and was exceptionally well attended. It was intended as a service of thanksgiving as well as a memorial and it is to be hoped everybody gave generously. In his speech, the vicar of Barnstaple, the Rev. Prebendary Wallington, alluded to the possible take over by the State — "if the hospitals become state hospitals there would be a great danger of official-dom; there would be a loss of that personal touch that means so much to the sufferers today, if that notice in front of the Infirmary "supported by voluntary contribution" should have to be removed. He was sure it would be an ill day for the sufferers that went there to be relieved."

As it was built

and as it ended

A time capsule placed under the foundation stone laid on 5th January, 1825, by Earl Fortescue has never been found. It contained coins of the reign of George IV and a scroll parchment which read;

"An edifice
By mercy and benevolence upreared
To lessen human misery. Here disease
Meets with a timely check, and rosy health
Again revisits the late pallid cheek.
Or if, in spite of human aid, stern death
Demand his victim, pity watches o'er
The humble suffer, calms his agony,
And smooths the rugged passage to the tomb."

Very comforting!

Over the years it had been altered and enlarged many times, and the original pleasant red brick facade had disappeared behind enlarged wards, balconies and large windows.

When, with mixed feelings, it closed in 1973, the NDI had five wards, with 105 beds, and also housed a nurses training school. It was sold to a developer for £85,000 and the site is now occupied by flats.

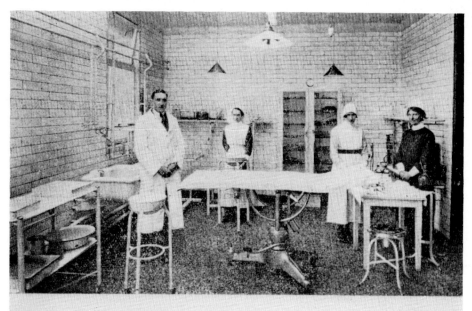

THE OPERATING THEATRE.

From the centenary booklet.

A later view showing the first extension.

SCENE FROM RIVER TAW SHOWING
TRINITY CHURCH, BARNSTAPLE.

Ilfracombe has lost its fair share of landmarks, some well loved, some not missed at all. Yet despite the passage of uncaring years when anything Victorian or Edwardian was deemed old-fashioned and pulled down to make way for the modern architecture of modern Britain, Ilfracombe has managed to retain much of its essential character.

The removal of all those brash plateglass shop fronts and the bright and flashing signs, would do much to return the harbour area to its nineteenth century state — but would today's holiday-makers prefer it thus?

And the High Street has not suffered nearly as much as in many towns who have had their hearts ripped out for car parks, new roads, and modern superstores. Perhaps suffering the economic doldrums for several decades will be seen to have been not such a bad thing if it has meant all this has passed Ilfracombe by. Looking at the old photographs and postcards it is surprising how much of the street is easily recognizable. It was still possible to have a traffic jam with horsedrawn carriages, and the advertisement signs hanging from the shops were almost as plentiful if not quite so colourful, and certainly not electrified. Now that its Victorian heritage has been placed in perspective, Ilfracombe's High Street is no longer the seedy, down at heart centre it was once branded. Far from it. Bright with intricate floral displays and thronged with visitors in the summer, it is all looking up in a most encouraging way. Perhaps as a next step some of the shops could be persuaded to return to the earlier style of shop front, and to take down the flashing signs?

Victorian days were good days, and why should the town not be proud of its heritage? Ilfracombe has lost the old market buildings and the shambles as have most of our towns. Gone, too, are the quaint, attractive, but most insanitary and cramped, little cottages and back-to-back streets, but the core of nineteenth century Ilfracombe remains with its good, solid architecture, its imposing villas, its promenades and terraces. Now that the fashion for decrying Victorianism is past, the town is capitalizing in a most refreshing manner and recalling with pride those days of its former and original glory in the reign of the Queen Empress.

It is sad therefore that two of the town's grandest pieces of Victorianism have vanished. Demolishing the *Ilfracombe Hotel* in 1976 was considered by many to be a piece of unforgiveable official vandalism. Certainly it robbed the town of its most imposing piece of high Victorian architecture. The demise of the pavilion happened gradually over the decades so that its loss was not so obvious. Only today, comparing the replacement with the original structure, can one assess that loss.

Once a building has gone, it becomes difficult to imagine it occupying what seems to be a hopelessly inadequate site. How could such a huge hotel have stood on the seafront where today are a few flowerbeds and lawns? Photographs show a truly enormous building. How ambitious our Victorian forebears were. No half measures. Think big. Build big. No cautious pussyfooting around with a small hotel to see if it would be successful. And how they moved — the hotel was built in just one year, opening in May 1867. It cost £14,944 with Carr Pethick of Plymouth the builders. It was 150 foot long by 80 feet deep, and contained 166 rooms, and the only areas not complete on opening day were the stables and coach houses.

Everything was built to a most luxurious standard. There was a billiard room, a smoking room for the men and a piano room for the ladies, with a magnificent dining room 80 feet by 36 feet and 22 feet in height. If that was too intimidating, all meals could be served in your own room, which connected by speaking tube direct with the bar! There were bathrooms and bedrooms specially designed for invalids, and it was recorded that the bedrooms on the first floor had brass bedsteads whilst those on the second and third had to make do with iron. Gas cylinders in the basement supplied 250 gas lights throughout the hotel, and the cellars contained vast quantities of wine in both casks and bottles, and casks of beer.

The staff had their own accommodation with a servants' hall, and a dining hall for the servants of the guests. The kitchen must have been most impressive with a 25 foot long kitchen range, an open range, and its own bake house. One wonders how much coal was needed to keep a constant supply of hot water, and how large

Two interior photographs of the Ilfracombe Hotel. The Dining Room, above, and the Palm Lounge taken around 1894. This later became the Free Library and Rest Room.

the boiler house was.

The tariff per day quoted at that time was:

Sitting room 4/- to 10/-
Bedrooms 1/6 to 5/- single
Double bedrooms 4/- to 6/-
Dressing rooms 1/6
Servants bedrooms 1/6
Breakfast 1/6 plain, 2/- meat, 2/6 ham & eggs, Bill of fare.
Breakfast 2/- Dinner 3/6 Servants day board 4/-
Fires 1/- to 1/6 per day Wax candles 1/- per day Gas 1/- per day
Baths 2/-, 1/- or 6d. Attention at bath 1/6
Attention at dinner 6d. Attention at breakfast 3d.

The hotel must have been hugely successful in those early years, for in 1871 a new wing was built, bringing the total number of rooms up to 250.

It would be interesting to see some of the guest lists for the hotel and know who patronised such a splendid establishment. It must have ranked many wealthy and titled people amongst its visitors, including Prince Wilhelm of Germany, the future Kaiser Bill, and first cousin to Edward VII. He came on several occasions before the First World War and became quite a familiar figure on the promenade.

The hotel was surrounded by its own pleasure grounds and private promenade, at the far end of which a covered swimming pool was erected. It was filled with sea water and only open to the public at certain hours during the day. This was badly damaged by the tidal wave in 1910.

The hotel made its first trading loss of £748 in 1925. In 1928 the first overtures were made to Ilfracombe Urban District Council, and it seemed all would go well with a purchase price of £43,500 agreed in February. By March, however, the council changed its mind and decided to rent the west wing, the swimming pool and the promenade and grounds for an annual rent of £1,250. The hotel company was left with the original hotel building and the gardens immediately in front.

War time came, and the hotel was requisitioned by the War Office, for use as RAPC offices.

The hotel in 1890

Finally in 1945 the UDC agreed to purchase the building. Part was leased as the Holiday Inn, and the west wing became council offices.

By 1974 the condition of the building was giving concern. The upper rooms (or attics) had been empty for thirty years, and inspections by the council's own officers declared them unsuitable for conversion to flats. An ambitious plan for a dance hall, solarium and bars with a market place was granted permission, but never came to anything.

Ilfracombe UDC gave way to the North Devon District Council. They were landed with a monstrous white elephant and could see no practical use for the building. They decided to demolish. The ensuing outcry must have surprised them. The hotel was immediately spotlisted as Grade II, which meant it could not be knocked down overnight, and a Public Inquiry was called. The council's report stated that there were many structural cracks, the bricks and mortar had weathered, in places to a depth of four inches. The roof leaked, the chimneys were in need of replacing, and parapets unsafe. Repairs were estimated at £550,000.

How attitudes change! The council's consultant architect did not consider the hotel of sufficient merit to warrant preservation. The polychrome work was the most important feature, he said, and would be extremely difficult to repair. He thought it (the hotel) 'visually undesirable'.

In his summing up, the inspector, with unusual sensitivity, said "I fully sympathise with the reluctance of local residents to accept the loss of a well-loved, familiar feature of marked character in the town centre — especially when other changes have occurred in recent years which have not always met with public approval — but the alternatives to granting listed building consent would not be in the public interest. An attractive seaside resort largely dependant on the tourist trade cannot gain from having a large, decaying, dangerous and empty building occupying a prime site in the town centre and blocking part of the limited seafront for an indefinite period. I am sure that the building will never be properly restored and it is for everyone's benefit to remove it now and use this site as a landscaped open space behind Wildersmouth Bay."

Ilfracombe Hotel was demolished in 1976.

The new Pavilion – before the zig-zag walk was constructed in 1892, and with the Wesleyan Church in the background and the lattice fence in the foreground – removed 1894.

The Victoria Pavilion still exists. A long low building sheltered from the sea by the Capstone Hill and envisaged as a place of entertainment for the visitors. So why is it included? Because the original Victoria Pavilion has vanished, replaced bit by bit until virtually nothing of the old glass house remains. Readers must judge for themselves which is the more attractive building.

The pavilion was built in 1887 to commemorate the Queen's silver jubilee. It cost around £6,000 and was hailed as "a structure of elegance and charm, built in the style of a miniature Crystal Palace", with the idea of providing visitors with somewhere to promenade on wet days. It was

"200 ft long, 45 ft wide and 40 ft high. The interior is ornamented with various flowering shrubs and climbing plants. Lavatories and

cloak rooms are provided. Outside, facing the lawn, seats have been placed protected by a glass covering. Smoking is allowed on this verandah, but not inside the Pavilion. No charge is made for admission except on a very few occasions, but collections are made by some of the concert parties who perform, and a charge is made for the best seats. Even a wet day may be made quite enjoyable in the Pavilion."

This description comes from a 1908 guidebook, and is accompanied by a photograph showing the pavilion, the bandstand and what appears to be an improvised theatre on the lawns behind the shops.

Concerts were given regularly inside the pavilion and the town band also performed almost daily during the season. It must have been an extremely pleasant building in which to while away a few hours and seems to sum up a more leisured age when visitors took care over their dress and appreciated somewhere to show off their elegance, and to meet their fellow visitors — truly a place in which to see, and to be seen.

Taken around 1930, the centre portion has been replaced, and the lawns developed.

Later it became known disparagingly as the cucumber frame. This unique glass and steel structure survived until the authorities decided they needed a purpose built concert hall with seating for large numbers. The old pavilion was alright for informal concerts, but quite unsuited to theatrical performances and variety shows. So in 1924 the central section was replaced with the structure we see today, or, as one contemporary account states —

> *"the centre of the old glass house was deleted and a new structure of steel and patent concrete blocks was inserted. Folding partitions gave access to the wings on either side. "*

Ultimately the wings were also replaced — and Ilfracombe lost a remarkable building.

The interior of the Pavilion.

Tors Pavilion

Admission – 1d. and 2d.   The path is private property; hence the charge.

At the west end of the town, approached on one side by steep roads and paths, and on the other rising abruptly from the sea, are six or seven hills, towering one above the other to a height of over 2600 ft. If the visitor sees nothing else of Ilfracombe, a view from the Tors will indelibly impress on the mind a remembrance of Ilfracombe scenery. The ascent is made by a series of zigzags, cut out of the side of the cliff, and the pathway is entered by a cottage in the Tors Park Road. The views from every turn of the path are magnificent. Seats are provided in plenty along the zigzag, and a refreshment pavilion awaits the thirsty at the summit.

This description comes from a guide book written at the turn of the century. The Tors have changed little since, except to gain an extra 'r' and to lose the admission charge. The pavilion on the summit, and the flagpole have also gone.

The Seven Hills, including the Tors Walks, were purchased by the National Trust in 1967 with Enterprise Neptune funds, and provide an incomparable area of fine walks and views. The coastal footpath climbs up out of the town and over the hummocky hills and on to Lee. There must be many heavily laden walkers who would be glad to stop at the Pavilion and refresh themselves after the steep haul. But the pavilion was demolished in 1964 and very few traces of it remain.

MEET OF EXMOOR FOXHOUNDS
MARCH 1934
A

Until 1970, the **Blackmoor Gate Hotel** was a well known rendezvous, situated at the meeting of the Barnstaple and Ilfracombe roads to Lynton and South Molton. It was a busy corner, with the railway station for the little Lynton railway on one corner, a petrol-filling station on another, and the hotel on a third. Now it is just a busy road junction, with the station turned into a public house, the petrol station demolished and replaced by a car park, toilets and a tourist information board, and an occasional cattle-auction held on the site of the hotel.

It was burnt down on the night of the 15th December, 1970, and five fire appliances tried unsuccessfully to put out the blaze. The 18-year-old barmaid, Susan Norman from Combe Martin, lost her life, as did two of the owner's Great Danes.

The hotel was in the process of being sold, and the purchaser, Mr Geoffrey Doven of Surrey, was in the bar having a drink with the owners, Mr & Mrs Edwin Griffin, when they noticed the fire. Mr Doven drove back to the farmhouse where he was staying to raise the alarm – presumably the hotel 'phone was already out of action – but the fire had too good a grip. The hotel had 22 bedrooms, and was a 2-storeyed flat-roofed building of unprepossessing design.

Somewhere close-by was the single-storey Broom's hotel and restaurant – and at one time a Mah Jong Chinese restaurant was also advertised at Blackmore Gate.

It may well be that in a few year's time *Caffyn's Golf Course* will no longer be a memory, but that a new up-to-date course will be resurrected on the ghost of the old.

Memories are dim as to the exact history, but it seems that it was first developed in the 1890's as a nine-hole course.

George Bowden was the green keeper for 41 years until he retired, aged 70, and his daughter recalls helping her mother with the cream teas served to the players in the little clubhouse. She remembers it as an 18 hole course, with ladies and gentlemen riding out from Lynton in their carriages. Apparently it was very popular with the visitors and local gentry, and the local lads did well out of their caddy fees. It seems that it was the First World War that put paid to this beautifully situated, if windy, little course, and it passed into the ownership of Lee Abbey. By the time this charming account was written in 1920 the sheep and the heather had taken over.

"Perhaps the confusion as to Martinhoe arose from the fact that Martin of Tours was at the time of the Conquest made overlord of the adjacent Combe Martin which thereby took his name. And Matta sleeps there now, I think, in his lonely mound on the height in full view of his unknown brother chief of Trentishoe Barrow.

Or was his tumulus cut into in the early nineties to make the little nine hole course which then came into existence? For links there were on the top of this moor and not such bad ones either, the greens being quite good. Stones formed the drawback, and if one got off the fairway, good-bye to your ball in the gorse and heather. The pro., I remember, had a clever little terrier who would retrieve out of the thickest roughty-toughty, and on a crowded links would have been a source of much profit to his master. But no one ever played here except ourselves, and the rare labourer who passed would eye our efforts in amaze and thus unburden his soul at night:

"Hev'e zeeen thiccy lil ole geame of jolf, Gaarge?"

"Noe, what like be 'un?"

"There be two as plays 'un, and one of 'un makes a lil heap of muck an' putts a lil ball op, and then her hits 'un – her hits 'un

as hard as ever her can. An' then they goes an' looks vor 'un. An' they looks an' they looks for most a half hour an' at last they vinds 'un. An' when hers vound 'un, whoy danged if doan't hit 'un again!"

It was a little known game in those parts then and not so long established in England. Indeed, I remember playing at Westward Ho! in 1880 when that course and Blackheath were the only two South of Tweed.

Well, the links are gone now; the sheep have demolished the bunkers and the greens have vanished under the all-conquering heather. Aesthetically the change is for the better. The little wooden pavilion stood on the road overlooking the sea towards Wales; the first two holes ran South and then crossed the road East, about half a mile from which point the Lynton links on Caffyns Down were situated. Thence the line returned to Martinhoe Cross where stood the fifth green closely guarded by two roads. One short hole to the West and then a straight long three to the home green.

Here I met once with a curious adventure. Teeing off from the fourth green I struck what was probably the finest drive I ever did in my life – a screamer, of low trajectory and heading for the pin. Visions of a hole in one crossed my mind. A hole it was, but of another kind, for to my horror at that identical moment over the brow of the road came a carriage and pair. In vain I invoked the High Gods. Straight into that carriage panel went that ball; the carriage stopped; there was a pause; the door flew open and out bundled an old gentleman, purple in the face, and advanced towards me. There was no covert so I had to face the music. Judge of my surprise when instead of the winged words I was expecting he offered profuse apologies for spoiling what he was good enough to term my magnificent drive! Sporting old boy! I made his better acquaintance afterwards.

It was pleasant up there even when things went adversely for one's ball. You must remember that in those days the amenities of the place were unspoiled; no little railway in the offing to disfigure the moor, no telegraph poles, no new roads to bring the traffic, but a glorious view of the sea and coast line with Wales occasionally visible in the far distance, though from the point of view of fine weather this was considered very undesirable.

On the night of August Bank Holiday Monday, 1913, an unexpected spectacular lit up the sky above Lynton. Residents and visitors alike gazed in astonishment as flames burst from the roof of *Hollerday House,* visible for miles around.

The large mansion had been built only twenty years previously on the steep hillside overlooking Lynton and the bay far below. It had been the home of Sir George Newnes, who had retired to Lynmouth in 1885 from a busy life in London as a newspaper proprietor and MP for Newmarket. He had become very much the local dignatory and public benefactor, being largely instrumental in the building of the Lynton to Barnstaple railway, and of the cliff railway linking Lynton to Lynmouth, and thus saving the steep toil uphill. In 1896 he received his baronetcy for "services to the Liberal Party and for producing clean, wholesome publications." His new residence was situated directly above the railway terminus, and some say he intended to have a private extension to Hollerday House. Lynton's impressive town hall was the gift of Sir George. He died in 1910.

A year after his death, this eulogistic account appeared in the local press.

"Of all the beauty spots dotted over this fair isle of ours, none can surpass in grandeur of scenery that part of the North Devon coast around Lynton. Here the cliffs attain a truly majestic height and are crowned by glorious moorland rising to an altitude of 800 feet, from which the eye can roam over so magnificent a stretch of country that it has earned for itself the right to be termed "The Switzerland of England." Upon almost the highest point of Lynton is perched that unique marine residence known as "Hollerday House," for some time the country seat of the late Sir George Newnes, which is now in the market by order of the executors. The house is one of the most perfectly appointed in the Kingdom, and affords accommoda tion for a fairly large establishment. In addition to stabling and motor garage and lovely pleasure grounds, the property carries two detached residences which are let and produce £105 per annum, a nice little offset against the upkeep of Hollerday House and the 40 acre which encompass it. The sale is advertised to take place at the Mart, E. C., on July 25th, by Hampton and Sons."

An early view, showing the young trees covering what had been a bare hillside.

Apparently the house, despite its glowing description, failed to sell. A further report states that no expense was spared in its erection, by local builder Mr Bob Jones, and estimates placed the final cost at around double the stated £9,000. Lady Newnes and her son, Sir Frank, sold the furniture and returned to London. The grounds were, the report states, held on a long lease by Sir George, and this and the house were subsequently acquired by Sir Thomas Hewitt, a great friend and neighbour of Sir George. He, too, offered the house for sale by auction, but again it was withdrawn. For such a magnificent property in such an unrivalled position, it can only be assumed that the asking price was excessive.

Then came the fire.

"The announcement of the destruction by fire of Hollerday House, the well known and beautiful summer residence of the late Sir George Newnes, has been read with much regret .... "

So reads a contemporary report. It continues that although no definite clue had been discovered, there could be little doubt that the fire was caused by suffragists. Sir George was the proprietor of 'Tit-Bits' — a much more respectable publication then than now, but still the target, perhaps of the feminists.

105

The flames were first spotted around 10.45pm and the Town
Crier was used to summon the fire brigade. This account of the fire
gives a graphic description of the problems of fighting a fire in the
early years of this century. It would seem there was little anyone
could do but watch ....

*Hollerday House occupied a position on the hill of that name, high above
any house in Lynton. Thus it was that, at about 10.45 p.m. on Monday night, when
sparks were seen rising above the building, followed by dense clouds of smoke and
tongues of flame, the alarm quickly spread. The public has always been privileged
to use the beautiful grounds adjoining the house, and it was not long before a huge
crowd assembled in the neighbourhood of the burning building. The members of the
Fire Brigade were summoned by the Town Crier, and were promptly on the scene,
under Capt Long, bringing with them their hose-reel. The fire was simultaneously
observed from several points, and one man aroused Mr. John Slee (the gardener),
who keeps the keys of the house, and who occupied the lodge house at the entrance
to the drive. Other early arrivals were P.C.'s Sparks and Hurford and Messrs.
Richards and Ralph. The hall door was forced, and it was immediately seen that
the flames had secured a good hold, for the massive oaken staircase, under which
the main outbreak appeared to have occured, was blazing furiously, while flames
were shooting up from the direction of a bath-room at the north end of the house,
where another outbreak had apparently started. The only supply of water available
was from a private reservoir at the rear, but, as this allowed of the use of only one
length of hose and the reservoir was situate on but a slightly higher level than the
mansion, it was seen that it would be impossible to save the building. However, with
one length of hose at their disposal the firemen did their best, and succeeded in
preventing the flames spreading to outbuildings, and also extinguished flames
which broke out among the trees and undergrowth in the woods adjoining.*

*Meanwhile, as time passed, the fire continued its destructive work in the
main building. Clouds of smoke, lighted up by golden-coloured and bluey shafts of
fire, belched upwards, floors were burnt through one after the other, and huge pieces
of masonry tottered and fell, crashing through floors and ceilings until the gaping
spaces, which had formerly been spacious rooms, gradually resolved themselves into
one fiery furnace. By a strange coincidence, the last room to be consumed was that
in which the late Sir George Newnes passed away. This room was situate on the
ground floor next to the billiard-room. The latter, owing largely to the efforts of ohe
Fire Brigade, was left almost undamaged. The great apertures were in the partition
walls, from one to the other of which stretched massive iron joints bent out of shape
by the heat and the falling masses of plaster and brickwork, while the basement was
filled with an indescribable collection of smoking debris, including bricks, mortar,
and stone, huge pieces of lead melted from the roof and troughs, and twisted pipe
lengths. Lying on edge of the ground in what had formerly been the scullery was a
bath which had crashed through the ceiling above. Practically all the woodwork –
which was such a feature of the oak-panelled hall – had been consumed, and the
paneless windows, blackened walls, and charred beams completed a scene of*

HOLLERDAY HOUSE, LYNTON

devastation. The only sign of life was the incessant chirping proceeding from a bird's nest on the ivy-covered outer wall of the hall, whose little occupants had escaped unscathed, while a weird sort of accompaniment to their twittering was provided by the wheezing of the chimney cowls which revolved above the gaunt walls of the ruined house. The Fire Brigade remained on the scene throughout the night, and the whole of next day, and until the gates were closed at mid-day, hundreds of sight-seers were attracted to the spot.

The accompanying photograph is interesting in that at first glance there appears to be nothing wrong with the house – a collection of gentlemen and ladies gathered in front – a garden party perhaps? And then the roofless state of the gables and towers becomes apparent – and perhaps the windows of the bay on the far left are without glass – but that would appear to be the sum total of the damage. The interior shots, issued later on a postcard, tell a different story however. The gardener/caretaker was insistent that he had locked up properly and that no-one had been allowed to enter. The report ends with the bald statement that although the house was lit by acetylene gas, the generator was empty.

The house remained, a burnt-out ruin, surrounded by its beautiful grounds, its tennis courts and walks, the carriage drives and plantations. In 1930 it was again offered for sale, this time by Harrods, who placed importance on the "profusely timbered grounds", and the "well-wooded valuable freehold", and the build-

VIEW FROM BILLIARD ROOM   ENTRANCE   CORRIDOR

Fire damaged inteior

ing site. In other words, it was a development potential and the 'Picturesque Ruins of the Residence of the late Sir George Newnes' are mentioned only briefly, in brackets, as being capable of being made into a Charming Residence.

The local people had always enjoyed the freedom of Hollerday Hill, and its outstanding position had been fully appreciated and made use of by many of them. North Walk extended from the heart of Lynton around the seaward side of the hill, giving magnificent views across the Bristol Channel to Wales, and back to the Foreland. The path continued to the Valley of Rocks, and is now part of the coastal footpath.

In April, of 1933 this valuable beauty spot became part of the possessions of the people of Lynton and Lynmouth for ever, when John Ward Holman, having purchased the Hollerday estate, gave it to the town. Apparently he stepped in because the council did not have the funds, and proved himself to be at least an equally generous benefactor as Sir George, although his name appears not to be commemorated in connection with his most generous gift.

Mr J W Holman, OBE was born at Glenthorne – in Somerset according to contemporary reports – and moved to Lynton where he first ran a grocery business. Surprisingly little is known, or recorded, about someone who was so prominent in the town's affairs, and whose open-handedness was legendary. He died on 19th March, 1936 at his residence, The Cottage, aged 84 and a batchelor.

At one time he was the owner of both the Queen's Hotel and the Valley of Rocks Hotel, and he appears to have supported most of the activities in the area, from a £50 donation towards the cost of a parking space for the Lynton and Lynmouth Golf Club in 1934, to the purchase and donation to the town of Hollerday Hill with 60 acres of grounds.

By 1955 the ruins of the old house were rapidly becoming a danger and an embarrassment. If the townsfolk were to be given free access, then something had to be done about the crumbling masonry before someone was killed. The Royal Marine Commandos from Instow were called in and saved the council £2,000 in demolition fees by blowing up the shell. It did not go easily. The first charge of 5lb had little effect, but the second, of 20lb, did the job so efficiently that flying stones and debris broke slates on nearby houses.

The site was then levelled, and only the carriage drives, the tennis court site and the many and confusing walks remained, plus the cottage now known as Honeypot Cottage, that was the former lodge.

Today the hill is much less densely afforested than it would have been, say, thirty years ago. By 1970 the trees, many of them Monterey pines, were dead or dying. Much felling has taken place, and much replanting, but this will take time to fill the gaps.

The whole of Hollerday Hill has become much more appreciated as an attraction, and as a unique backdrop to the town of Lynton, and although the footpaths are not well signposted from the town itself, once the visitor has ventured onto the hill there is no hindrance to his wanderings. What is completely lacking, however, is any form of information as to the history of the strange plateaus, the numerous walks and drives, the sudden clearings, upon which he stumbles. Planners of walks these days seem to think everyone is interested only in the wildlife, and that man's hand is without importance and not worthy of a mention.

Lynton suffered another major loss when the *Royal Castle Hotel* burnt down in 1987. This huge Victorian block had dominated the skyline for over a hundred years – and there are some who say Lynton is the better off without it. It would have been a major asset to the town if this wonderful level site with its panoramic views over Lynmouth and across the Bay could have been left as a pleasure ground for locals and visitors to enjoy. But apparently the site is too valuable and there is a proposal to build flats. Apart from the grounds of the remaining portion of the Castle, only the churchyard gives visitors the chance to enjoy the wonderful views.

According to Pevsner, the hotel was built as a private house around 1810 "in a glorious position high above and overlooking the sea." It is described as a modest long white house, and the hotel which was added as "High to late Victorian, i.e. from the grimness of some of Ilfracombe and Westward Ho! to the heavy-handed gaiety of fancy tile-hanging and turrets and gables with woodwork painted white."

The earliest postcard shows the original house, with its attractive stone entrance porch and flanking french windows, entirely dominated by the high hotel addition. Also shown are the three entrance pillars, the central one of which disappeared to make more room for motor charabancs. Originally the hotel could provide stabling for around 100 horses, but it embraced the motor trade very early on, and most of the early postcards stress the availability of the motor garage, and 'Pratt's Motor Spirit'.

THE . . .
ROYAL CASTLE HOTEL,
LYNTON.

The LEADING HOTEL, standing in its own Grounds of 9 acres, facing the Sea.
Lighted throughout by Electricity.

Motor Garage.
Pratt's Motor Spirit.

Telegraphic Address—
" Castle, Lynton."

Later development shows a much altered hotel wing. The whole façade has been gothicised, with moulding round the much enlarged windows, a higher roof line, now castellated, and a mansard roof with dormer windows. The original building has also acquired a few additional bays and verandahs. Later on again, the whole thing has become covered in creeper.

In its heyday, the Castle was the premier hotel of the area, and the final accolade came when the young Edward VII, as Prince of Wales, stayed at the hotel in September, 1856, whilst visiting the area. Since then it became known as the 'Royal Castle' – and the existing hotel has many interesting photographs and mementos of those days.

But as with most large hotels, it fell on hard times. After the War, when part was used as an officer's mess, its fortunes gradually declined. The famous sprung dance floor was used as a roller skating rink. The original Morris wallpapers were emulsioned, or covered with artex, the panelling was removed or damaged, and the rooms cut around and altered. As so often happens, the hotel changed hands many times, each owner with new ideas and plans, but nothing could repair its tarnished image, and a long purse would have been needed to restore the hotel to its original glory, even if it was thought it would have been viable

One owner sought permission to demolish, but the whole was a listed building, and English Heritage withheld their consent.

Then came the fire.

Fortunately the original house was untouched, and the later wing built at right-angles onto the rest of the damaged structure. The current owner has managed to restore the atmosphere of the late regency era to the Royal Castle – not always easy when Health and Safety precautions have to come first, and perhaps it is the better for the removal of its overlarge neighbour.

So much has vanished from *Lynmouth* that a whole book could be filled with the sad tale of its losses.

But for Lynmouth the story is different. The losses have not been gradual. They are not the result of the passage of time, of decay, of redevelopment, which has been the story elsewhere. It was one night in August, 1952 that caused the damage. The devastating Lymouth Flood where the waters of the two rivers rose so quickly to such an unprecedented level that buildings and bridges all along the banks were swept away. That story is told elsewhere, and the photographs of the shattered village are many and well known. Yet some of the smaller buildings and structures are in danger of being forgotten. Some have never been replaced; such as the Middleham Cottages and the hydro-electric plant. Some have been rebuilt and strengthened, such as the bridge to Watersmeet, now curving high above the East Lyn, and the approach bridge carrying the main A39. This replaced Lyndale Bridge, a sturdy stone bridge, built in the mid 19th century which managed to withstand the fury of the flood whilst all around it collapsed, and its subsequent demolition was the cause of bitter controversy, not least from Mr Tom Bevan a former mayor of Lynton whose family had built the bridge in 1860, and whose name was recorded on a plaque in the centre of the bridge.

Although the bridge had survived, Mr Bevan's hotel adjoining it, had not. He was the owner of the Lyndale Hotel, a solidly built structure that somehow managed to bear the brunt of the waters and remain standing, although so damaged it was beyond repair. After that long night when he, his family and guests sat, and listened and waited, alone in the darkness amidst the roaring of waters, he wrote this account:

> *"The summer of 1952 had been notable for its thunderstorms and long rainy periods. Apart from a few spells of fine weather, the general conditions had been wet since mid-June. Consequently the ground, especially on the high moors, was waterlogged. The week*

prior to August 15th had been relatively fine, and the fatal day dawned with the promise of good weather. It was the last day of their holiday for many of the Hotel's forty odd guests, and there was talk at breakfast time of a farewell picnic together.

It must be pointed out here that in 1952 we were still under the influence of post war restrictions, and many visitors were still travelling by train and coach .... the mass use of motor cars was yet to come .... foreign travel was only for the few .... meat and sugar were still rationed. As the majority of the Hotel guests had been regular visitors since the war, the general atmosphere was more of a club than an Hotel. Ironically, that very morning, a "round robin" was presented to the office asking that we open for Christmas! At about 10 o'clock, the weather changed, the sun became overcast and slight rain began to fall. There was little or no wind, and the Barometer was steady. By mid-day, it had become gloomy and wet and by three o'clock was raining in torrents.

In order to follow subsequent events, it must be noted that the Hotel was built on the Victorian principal of basements .... the "ground" floor consisting of all the Public rooms being some ten feet above street level. Below were the kitchen store rooms and wine cellars, with the public bar built on to the rear, over which was the billiards room. Beyond the public bar were the garages and outbuildings, part of the latter containing staff flats.

The first indication of anything abnormal came at about 3.30pm when the street gullies choked and water poured into the basement. This had happened before during heavy thunderstorms, and as usual was tackled with mops and buckets. The East Lyn River, which ran alongside was now discoloured and beginning to rise, but to no great extent. One guest put up his fishing rod and was off to make the best of it, rain or no rain. By 5 o'clock, the rain had eased and we felt that we had won the 'battle of the buckets', but by 6 o'clock, it became obvious that we were in for something unusual. The river was well above its normal flood level by the time Dinner was served at 7pm, and was coming down in a black mass, as opposed to its usual brown, but was still well within its banks. After dinner, I drove my two children, daughter aged 13 and son aged 9, together with a guest and his daughter to the sea front Pavilion Concert party and noticed nothing amiss. On returning

An early view of The Lyndale Bridge *and the* Lyndale Hotel.

The opposite view after the floods.

Interior views of the hotel.

to the Hotel, I parked my car in the garage and was called downstairs by the Chef because the water was coming through the basement windows, flooding the kitchens. At the same time, the river began to flow around the rear of the Hotel taking with it some empty beer barrels from the back of the public bar. We realised that the position was getting serious, and that there was no question of baling out this time.

We "drew" the Aga and boiler fires, switched off the refrigerators and commenced to save whatever we could from the store cupboards, by passing the goods upstairs. My immediate thought was of the wine cellar with its precious contents, but alas, it was too late. The door was jammed, and we had to beat a hasty retreat to the stairs to save ourselves. By now, the water was waist deep, even so, we were quite satisfied that only the basement would be flooded so rang the fire brigade for help. They could not come to us as they were on their way to a call from Barbrook. At this stage, we were wondering what we could give the guests for breakfast! The electricity supply had now failed owing to the flooding of the power station then situated alongside the river. It was decided that I should fetch the children back from the Pavilion so attempted to make my way down the main street and was soon foundering in deep water. The West Lyn River was making a clean sweep over the roadbridge, between The West Lyn Cafe and the Lyn Valley Hotel, and about this time, the bridge completely disappeared. Being unable to continue by this route, I made my way up the hill towards Lynton, along the upper path known as Mars Hill Way, down to the sea front. An anxious crowd was gathered in pitch darkness and pouring rain and from them I learnt that every boat in the harbour had been washed out to sea. With other local people, I organised a "chain", and made our way back along Mars Hill Way.

We advised all who were able, to proceed up to Lynton and I led my own party back to the Hotel, still feeling that there was no immediate danger some having decided to return via the main street. It was now that the first tragedy occurred, two people were washed away.

After wading through about a foot of water outside the building, our party reached the Hotel safely. By now the garage at the rear was completely flooded; one guest had rescued his car and *driven up to Lynton to raise the alarm that we were cut off. The last to leave the garage was a local girl who rescued her pony from a loose box stable. Thoughts then turned to the bars at street level, both were awash to the tops of the counters and the attempts to save the cash tills were without success.*

We were completely marooned but still only by the East Lyn River, which appeared to have reached its peak. So far as the adjoining houses and we were concerned, it was now that disaster struck. Hitherto, the West Lyn River had continued its course to the sea, taking away the front of the Lyn Valley Hotel plus part of the West Lyn Cafe opposite. As I previously mentioned, the street bridge had been washed away and now also the block of houses comprising "Riverside", "The Falls" and the Granville Hotel were taking a severe hammering. All this time, however, debris was piling up under the solid concrete Prospect Bridge at the bottom of Lynton Hill.

This Bridge had originally been of light construction and as such, would most certainly have been washed away, but during the "Thirties", it had been widened in solid concrete, and no provision made for a larger arch. Consequently it held back the debris of trees, rocks, etc. which piled up and up preventing the river from flowing freely. With a terrific roar, the water burst over the right bank bringing its whole force plus boulders directly towards the Hotel. In its path, it demolished the Glen Lyn Filling Station, the Baptist Chapel, a house and shop property and also the corner of Shelly Cottage Guest House was torn off, finally completely flooding our ground floor.

Three people from the shop, a man, his wife and another woman were washed against the hotel; two were rescued through the lounge window whilst the other was washed on to the roof of the saloon bar and through the office window. We ordered everyone upstairs trying to save what we could as we went, I did succeed in opening the office safe to rescue its contents. An attempt to save the Cocktail Bar till failed, and this was where we suffered our only casualty, a budgerigar.

The swing doors of the front hall burst open, a solid wall of water and debris poured in and on its crest was noted, of all things, a child's wellington boot! At the same time, a similar wall of water

The Lyndale Hotel and Bridge, plus proprietor fishing

invaded the office and cocktail bar, pouring through the building into the East Lyn River alongside which was still below floor level. The ground floor was now a raging torrent, with furniture plus debris which included small trees, crashing about in all directions. Adjoining houses were similarly affected and all occupants had to beat a hasty retreat upstairs. Our Chef's wife and children were trapped in their flat over the garage, but were resuced by a local man who guided them with his own children to an adjoining house.

The noise had become deafening due to the rocks and debris from the West Lyn River being piled against the south wall of the Hotel, up to the height of the first floor bedroom windows, and the water was actually seeping on to the landing. It was now "everyone up to the second floor".

At this moment, the largest bedroom in the front of the hotel collapsed under the strain, allowing everything to drop into the flooded lounge beneath. This made us think of the rear wing, in which our own bedroom was situated, as being vulnerable. With one of our staff, I went to see if it were possible to save any of our personal belongings. As we entered the room, we saw the outer wall which overlooked the East Lyn, gradually subsiding. We grabbed what we could and retreated just before the wall disappeared. Shortly afterwards there was a terrific crash and the whole wing went.

Until now, there had been no sign of panic, but the crash and subsequent vibration caused a murmur of fear which we quickly had to subdue. After this, everyone was remarkably cool and collected and we had the feeling that the worst was over.

Taking stock of our position, we numbered forty five men, women and children. We were completely cut off from outside help by the raging waters and we knew that only the south-facing wall stood between us and the total collapse of the building. All the light we had were a few candles, no water to drink and only a few sweets and biscuits which were shared between us. We had salvaged a bottle of brandy and a bottle of sherry from the cocktail bar, but alas, the kitchen porter had found the sherry, finished it off and was flat out on the floor. The brandy was rationed out to those who needed it.

We signalled SOS with torches to the hill opposite where we could see lights moving, but realising they could do nothing for us, tried to make the best of things by settling down in the bedrooms and on the landing. The people rescued from the shop earlier on had been put to bed, and it was here that a touch of humour crept in when a young lady visitor exclaimed "there is a man in my bed – I've been waiting years for this to happen!"

The hours passed slowly and by early morning, the water was definitely falling. At about 5 o'clock, dawn broke and we were able to see the rocks piled against the south wall of the hotel and wondered how much of old Lynmouth remained to be seen.

Suddenly we saw lights approaching from the direction of Watersmeet Road and heard voices, then it was not long before PC Harper and members of the Fire Brigade scrambled through one of the first floor bedroom windows enabling us to make our first contact with the outside world. They had come over Summerhouse Hill from Barbrook, so were able to give us the news of the tragedy which had occured at that little hamlet.

Their first job was to bring into our comparative safety those marooned in the house opposite, namely Mrs and Miss Sheppard, the Chef's wife and two children, all of whom had spent the night in one room which had only been supported by one brick wall. In the light of day it could be seen that they had had a miraculous escape. After holding a roll call, we considered what to do for the best and decided that someone should try to reach the Tors Hotel by way of the Lyndale Bridge adjacent to our hotel as this was still intact, in order to obtain transport if possible, to seek help from Porlock. Owing to the disruption of the telephone wires, Porlock which is just over the Somerset border knew nothing of the disaster at this time. PC Harper undertook this task and was successful in reaching there by car to break the news.

It was by now light enough to see, and a fantastic sight met our eyes .... the West Lyn had completely changed course and was pouring down what had been the road to Lynton, across the front of the hotel and on to the Lyndale Bridge .... the whole of the valley was a mass of rocks and debris .... the Chapel with house and shop adjoining had completely disappeared .... the corner of the Shelley Guest House had been sheared off .... the first house of the Granville block was half demolished .... the front of the Lyn Valley Hotel had

The Hall.

The Hotel before the corner turret was added – showing the rear wing built on the bank of the Lyn.

been carried away as had the Rhenish Tower overlooking the harbour, the Beach Hotel plus the old Lifeboat House and Institute.

Strangely enough, the group of houses forming Lynmouth Street though flooded, were structurally intact.

After jamming the Prospect Bridge, the West Lyn had come down with such force, throwing its whole weight against the hotel, then against the Manor Grounds where it had eaten in to a depth of 50 yards, carrying away the avenue of chestnuts and Silex oaks. It had then rebounded across to the Beach Hotel and through the harbour. There is little doubt that had the Prospect Bridge collapsed the whole of Lynmouth Street including the Granville block would have been destroyed with possible heavy loss of life whilst the hotel plus adjoining properties would have been spared.

It now seemed advisable to abandon the building in case of further collapse as we had no idea as to the state of the foundations, but we knew that the rear wing which included six bedrooms, billiards room and public bar, had completely disappeared as had the garage buildings and outside staff quarters. Slowly everyone filed out of a first floor bedroom window on to the slippery rocks and debris carrying the smaller children in blankets. The church appeared to offer our first sanctuary, but even here there was a foot of water, despite its higher level, so the neighbours gradually absorbed us into their homes and provided us with food and shelter. This was a considerable undertaking because not only did they do it for our company, but also for all the occupants of the other houses which had been washed away. Upstream from the hotel, 18 cottages and houses had disappeared including the whole hamlet of Middleham with the loss of seven lives, five adults and two children, and we were yet to hear of further tragedies.

Together with all those above the river junction, we were completely isolated as the road to Lynton was cut off by the West Lyn, and the Watersmeet Road was impassable at Hillsford Bridge. All services were completely disrupted but rescue workers were beginning to arrive across the still raging rivers, and this enabled us to signal to them that we had no casualties but needed food and water.

Knowing that all my company was temporarily housed, I then returned to the hotel to reassess the position. Further examination *revealed that we also had had a very narrow escape. The South wall which had taken such a battering by the hundreds of tons of rocks was cracked in two places .... had this collapsed nothing could have prevented the entire building from being swept out to sea.*

The relief of knowing we had survived was enormous, but in spite of this, the damage was heartbreaking. The lounge, office, front hall, cocktail bar and smoking room lounge were completely gutted. Every piece of furniture was smashed to resemble match-wood, including four tallboys filled with precious china, antiques and books.

The Dining room on the East Lyn side was a fantastic sight. Although it had escaped the rush of debris, it was flooded to a depth of several feet, but in spite of this, some of the tables were still standing with the cloths and silver intact. It was obvious that the other cloths and silver had been swept through the french windows into the East Lyn.

The force of the water was illustrated by the heavy safe from the office being carried across the hall into the dining room and by the hall having an entire small tree plus a large Victorian sofa from another house in its midst. The remains of the still room and pantry next to the dining room hung crazily over the river, most of the contents having slipped away. The kitchens and the whole of the basement were filled with rubble as were the wine cellar and staff rooms.

By mid-morning, although still isolated, all kinds of help was arriving in the form of troops, police and Red Cross workers from the Lynton and Somerset areas. When links were established with the Lynton and Countisbury sides, it was found possible to cross the Lyndale Bridge on foot, through the hotel upstairs and out of the bedroom windows, much to the detriment of the remaining landing and bedrooms carpets! This gave us an exit route to Somerset. By mid-day it became evident that Lynmouth must be evacuated owing to the destruction of essential services, therefore a coach shuttle service was laid on to Minehead, starting from the entrance to the Beacon half way up Countisbury Hill. The visitors were the first to be sent smoothly away then came the turn of those residents like ourselves, who were cut off from Lynton. It was a hard decision to make as we had to leave our homes open to the world. We were promised police protection for them in our absence, but this later proved to be quite inadequate.

We were a motley crowd who arrived late in the evening at the Minehead Cinema ballroom which had been turned into a receiving station. Most of us were in the same clothes in which we had spent a sleepless night, some our own, others borrowed but all of us tired and hungry. Two people especially spring to my mind, my daughter clinging desperately to her spaniel with whom she had spent the night huddled together for warmth, and the other, our small sized Chef in a RNLI jersey and trousers far too big for him. The people at Minehead were extremely helpful in providing us with hot drinks and food, and those visitors who could travel on home were given priority on the railway.

We local people were provided with coaches to return to Lynton but this proved a nightmare journey over washed out roads, also a detour had to be made via Dulverton, Brayford and Blackmore Gate to our destination.

At Lynton we found everything well organised, despite the lack of electricity and water, and after reporting to the town hall, we were allocated to various homes.

Tired and weary, we wished for nothing else but bed.

Thus concluded 24 hours of an experience, which those of us who went through it, are never likely to forget.

Lynmouth Tors Park Villas

The Hydro Electric Building is on the right.

Necessity, it has always been said, is the mother of invention, and the people of Lynmouth and Lynton have proved exceptionally capable of overcoming the problems of living in such a remote and difficult-of-access spot. In some cases they were in advance of the rest of the country, and the *hydro-electric* scheme is a good case in point. Many parts of Devon did not receive the benefits of electricity until well into the 20th century, but Lynton and Lynmouth were lit up in 1890.

In March of that year the generating station opened, and worked without ceasing until it was washed away in the 1952 floods. The first ever generating plant had come into operation only eight years previously.

The originator of the scheme, Mr C Geen, had originally envisaged lighting the streets and public areas only of the two towns, but in 1892 the Devon & Cornwall Bank and the bank manager's house, were connected. Mr Geen's company, the Devon Electric Light Company, sold out to Mr H H Benn, and in 1894 a new company, the Lynton and Lynmouth Electric Lighting Co. came in to being, the two directors being Mr Geen and Mr Benn.

It was soon realised that the summer flow of water in the East Lyn was inadequate to generate sufficient power for the two villages and in 1895 the engineers ingeniously solved the problem. A reservoir was built high up on Summerhouse hill with a fall of 760 feet. Day-time electricity pumped water up, and at night it rushed back down through a six inch pipe to drive twin Pelton wheels, boosting power from the conventional turbines.

Demand was constantly rising and in 1921 two oil-fired engines were installed to supplement the water power.

The plant produced 110 volt electricity, as opposed to the national grid 240 volts, and at the time of the floods SWEB had taken over the system and were in the process of standardising it.

All that now remains is the carefully constructed leat that carried water from a point higher up the East Lyn to feed the turbines and it was one man's constant job to keep the leaves from choking the grating.

Lynrock Water, and 'Sparklynrock' were two of the natural products that bubbled up on the banks of the East Lyn, and were bottled by the *Lynrock Natural Mineral Water Syndicate*. Memories are vague as to exactly when the little bottling plant was built, or who first had the bright idea of utilising this valuable natural asset, but many people still remember the colourful Mr C D Attree.

Under his direction the fame of the Lynrock Water spread far and wide, and the brochure he produced gives a Cannon Street, London address and also agents in Liverpool and Bristol. The Chief Depot was Lynton "where all Empties must be sent to."

Of course in those days Lynton was part of the railway network, and Mr Attree and his model T Ford pick-up truck were a familiar sight, carrying his products to the station for transmission to the rest of the country — and perhaps even abroad as he had offices in the two largest ports of the day.

Mr Attree was an enterprising gentleman; he also owned and ran the Falls Tea Rooms that stood at Watersmeet below the road, and at Myrtleberry, his home, there was also a tea garden.

Lynrock Mineral Water spring.

LYNMOUTH. FALLS CHALET   86237.

Many people still remember the monkeys he kept there — fed, no doubt, on best cream teas by the visitors. He was at one time a member of the local council.

At some time before the last War, Billy Cook took over and ran the bottling plant until he left around 1935. After the war only a small, sporadic operation was continued, until all was swept away in the 1952 flood — which also took Mr Attree's tea rooms.

The water is still there, its pure taste and refreshing qualities available free of charge to all who walk up the left bank of the East Lyn, and notice the plaque and bottle stump embedded in the rock beside the spring.

Also lost in the floods was the bridge to Watersmeet, since replaced

"An ugly modern building, badly planned and worse built."

House design is one field where individual taste has had almost unlimited scope, especially in the days before planning consent, when the only limitations were one's purse. Some quite extraordinary properties have been built by eccentric owners, or those with more pretentions than good taste, but outstanding, in North Devon at least, must have been *Welcombe House,* and this was the verdict of a Welcombe resident who kept a fascinating scrapbook of the locality.

It is hard to visualise this strange, square, flat-roofed edifice standing on the ridge of high ground, no more than a mile from the cliffs.

According to the newspaper clipping of 22nd March, 1929, Welcombe House had been built not many years before by Mr W P Skynner of Marsland, Bideford, and consisted of some 16 rooms. It had been bought two years previously by a local farmer, Mr J Gifford, of South Hole, Hartland who intended converting it into a private hotel. However, it was burnt down almost completely in the early hours of Sunday morning:

> *"It was partly furnished, no one was living there at the time. The damage, mounting to several thousand pounds, is said to be covered by insurance. A skittle match was played in an adjoining alley the night before, but this was not damaged. The cause of the outbreak is a mystery."*

The house was subsequently demolished, and a new, single storey property of strange design erected on the site, also called Welcombe House. The entrance pillars would appear to be the only tangible remains, although no doubt much of the building material for the existing Welcombe House came from the burnt-out shell.

Nearby is a property of similar design, and equally out of keeping with its surroundings, known as Berry Park. It is popularly believed locally that this was the sister building to Welcombe House, incorporating staff quarters, dower house and an old an cottage – the only original part of the whole scenario. The Walker family, of Johnny Walker whisky fame, are said to be the builders of both properties, to whom the Skynner's were related, and in Welcombe church there are several memorials to both families. Unfortunately all trace of the history of these two remarkable houses seems lost, and the only contemporary photograph to come to light is that accompanying the press clipping, showing the ground floor windows boarded up.

Acknowledgements

Much time has been spent closely scrutinising old newspapers, books, journals and papers, but particular thanks go to the staff of the North Devon Record Office and Library at Barnstaple, and to the Atheneaum without which this book would have been immeasurably the poorer, if not impossible. The Ilfracombe Museum – dear Joy Slocombe – supplied many of the photographs and information on Ilfracombe; Bideford Library; Braunton and Lynton Museums and libraries; the Bideford Archive and Pat Slade were invaluable. Appledore RNLI lent the lifeboat house photo and this, and many others owe their clear reproduction to the photograhic skills of Sandra Yeo. Private individuals gave unstintingly of their time, their memories, and their precious photographs, and I consider their generosity a great privilege. I have decided not to name them to spare them any further pestering, which may be channelled through the author! For numerous cups of tea and coffee, patient listening and willingness to search for elusive information or photographs I am deeply grateful – and finally, I hope all those who helped have gained some measure of enjoyment. I know I have – and I hope those of you who now sit at leisure and enjoy the fruits of our labours will do likewise.

Brief Bibliography
North Devon Journal Herald
Bideford Gazette
Western Morning News
North Devon Clay – M J Messenger
Old Bideford – M J Goaman
Ward Lock Guide Books
Christie Estate papers
North Devon Anthology